Her

Revisited

Praise for *Herding Cats Revisited*

Many thanks for letting us see your updated volume. It is full of EVEN MORE insight and wisdom! Many congratulations.

Mark Dodgson – Emeritus Professor, University of Queensland, Australia

Sheridan Ash – Director, PricewaterhouseCoopers LLP, UK

Reading this new edition was a most enjoyable task. The additional material is very fresh and relevant and I chuckled frequently at the many incisive observations made by both yourselves and your contributors.

Ian Steadman – formerly Dean of Arts, University of the Witwatersrand, RSA; and Director of Development at the Open University and at Oxford Brookes University, UK

In an era of hype and inflated claims about the secrets of successful leadership, Herding Cats Revisited *bucks the trend by delivering the distilled, hard-earned experience of individuals who have led with high impact in the unbridled world of research and academia. The genius is that it actually provides a much broader roadmap for leading in 'today's' crazy world of work. A must read, reflect and apply.*

Ian Dean - International leadership coach, Stellenbosch, RSA

Usually, I am not drawn to books about work ethics or strategy, perhaps because I am instinctively inclined to learning from the school of hard knocks. But in this case, I ... found an easy how-to guide that covers absolutely every aspect of an effective career in academic teaching, research and leadership. It's a lifetime of learnings laid out, coming one after another like tasty morsels in a degustation menu. It's a way to graduate from the school of hard knocks without suffering the pain.

Alan Finkel - formerly Chief Scientist, Government of Australia and Chancellor, Monash University, Australia

...and for its predecessor, *Herding Cats*, when it was first published in 2010

This short book is lively, good fun but full of wisdom, eminently readable, great common sense and filled with really good quotes... a useful roadmap for any leader embarking on this tough enterprise.

Sir Gustav Nossal, FRS, University of Melbourne, Australia

I loved Herding Cats *– the 12 Cs are a terrific organizing principle; the manuscript is exuberant which is a great achievement as sometimes the topic can be disheartening for people setting out...A wonderful read.*

Prof. Mandy Thomas, formerly Pro Vice Chancellor, Australian National University

After reading Garrett and Davies' excellent little book, the aspiring university leader will know that s/he has to be: accountable, balanced, confident, decisive, ethical, fearless, generous, hard-working, imaginative, joyful, knowledgeable, likeable, mature, non-egotistical, optimistic, prudent, quick, reliable, scholarly, tenacious, unflappable, versatile, witty, xenian (it means hospitable), young at heart, and zestful. (An A to Z of herding practical cats, with apologies to Old Possum.)

Prof. Sir David Watson, formerly Vice-Chancellor, University of Brighton and Principal, Green Templeton College, Oxford, UK

I have just finished reading Herding Cats – it's a masterpiece! I think the lessons are applicable to our day-to-day life as well and I must say that this book is the mantra for 'the way of life'!

Sushil Borde, research engineer, Pune, India

Garrett and Davies have done a great job pulling together insightful anecdotes and quotes in an interesting and original framework. I am sure this book will become a handy companion to scientific texts on the bookshelves of senior managers in our learned institutions. It will definitely be on mine.

Dr Alex Zelinsky, Group Executive, CSIRO, Australia

This book is great!... It makes great common sense and is good reading for a broad spectrum of people – not only academics... I think King Solomon could not have done a better job.

Dr Stephen Akers, Consultant, Mollis, Switzerland

I am most impressed by the insights gathered. While an evening across the table from a wise man may be better than a month of study, it takes two to make a conversation worthwhile. The authors have proved great conversationalists, generously attributing wisdom to those they interview when it is the questions asked, and the integration of the answers, that makes this work so intriguing and worthwhile.

Prof. Glyn Davis, Vice-Chancellor, Univ. of Melbourne, Australia

A nice piece of valuable thinking! This book should reach all leaders and managers in academia!

Dr Erkki Leppavuori, President and CEO, VTT Technical Research Centre, Finland

I've used your little book on many occasions for the right individuals, a great way of sending a message and always a buzz when I see the light bulb go on!!

Bob Gee, Deputy Police Commissioner, Queensland, Australia

This book is a valuable addition to our understanding of leadership in the research environment. So much of value, drawn from deep experience, is packed into a pithy text, with the use of concepts and language that academics and researchers can relate to – so often a problem with 'management' texts.

Prof. Sharon Bell, Melbourne Graduate School of Education, University of Melbourne, Australia

I just want to say to you that your book is very well received by the scientific community, namely the Institute and Lab Directors and scientific administrative people. It is my hope that it will help enhance scientific management in China.

Jinghua Cao, Deputy Director, Bureau of International Cooperation, Chinese Academy of Sciences, Beijing (on the Mandarin version)

I have just been reading Herding Cats. *It is fantastic. So much wisdom and so relevant. A great book.*

Dr Clare Nourse, Associate Professor, Faculty of Paediatrics, University of Queensland, Australia

Thank you very much for your wonderful book… It has given me more insight into how to approach my current position. I think it is a must read for academic administrators.

Prof. Mkhululi Lukhele, Head of Dept of Orthopaedics, University of the Witwatersrand, Johannesburg, RSA

Herding Cats *is absolutely well done. This was no minor undertaking… the focus of the book is quite obviously very practical and down to earth.*

Dr Rich Adams, Senior Vice President, Battelle, USA

Thank you! I have just finished my first read of Herding Cats. *Magnificent – many aspects resonated. I will recommend it to my 5 leadership mentees! We also have 'enduring questions' sessions – I will make it the focus on a coming one.*

Peter Tugwell, Professor of Medicine, Univ. of Ottawa, Canada

I am not sure if Herding Cats *has gone to a second edition yet but we have decided to make a bulk purchase of 50 in the first instance with the idea of giving a copy to new VCs when they take up the post or for visitors.*

Prof. John Wood, Secretary General, The Association of Commonwealth Universities, UK

While I was recently acting for [the Secretary and our CEO], I saw your book on her desk so I took it home and read it. I really enjoyed it and have now recommended it to everyone I know.

Sandra Parker, Deputy Secretary, Workplace Relations and Economic Strategy, Dept. of Employment, Government of Australia

You will be glad to know that Herding Cats *is one book that has survived my cull before the move!*

The Hon. Ian Walker, Minister for Science, IT, Innovation and the Arts, State Government of Queensland, Australia

Herding Cats Revisited

Being more advice for aspiring
academic and research leaders

Geoff Garrett and Graeme Davies

Published in this first edition in 2021 by:

Triarchy Press
Axminster, UK
www.triarchypress.net

A catalogue record for this book is available from the British
Library.

ISBNs:
Print: 978-1-913743-35-2
ePub: 978-1-913743-36-9
PDF: 978-1-913743-37-6

Cover artwork: Walter Pichler

Printed by TJ International, Padstow, Cornwall

Cats will not be commanded
and
can choose their owner

Valeria Manferto De Fabianis (ed.)
Cats
(White Star Publishers, 2007)

For Janet and Svava –
caring and staunch supporters throughout all our
professional ups and downs

CONTENTS

Authors' Foreword

Over much of the fifty years we have known each other, we have enjoyed trading war stories around what we have learned, and observed, about the business of managing/ leading academic and research institutions – effectively, and otherwise. As a consequence, we committed ourselves to the discipline of putting pen to paper in terms of a small 'guidebook' for aspiring (and practising) leaders in our work-world.

It is well known that most academics and researchers like to exercise as much independence as possible in their professional lives. So in offering advice, somewhat tentatively, around leading and 'managing' academics and researchers, the well-known idea of 'herding cats' seemed to us an appropriate metaphor.

As a central part of the process of creating this book, we recognised that it would be extremely valuable to tap into the wisdom and experience of a number of the senior leaders around the world with whom we have interacted over the years, and whom we have admired. From their responses, coupled with our own perspectives, we realised that we might pull together some 'key lessons' that could be worth recording, and sharing.

To this end we posed a series of questions to them, along the lines of…

- What do you know now that you wish you had known 'back then', when you commenced – or got immersed in – your leadership career?

- If you are mentoring a new leader – a head of department, a dean, a programme manager – what would you wish to share, concisely, about 'operations'?… about 'strategy'?

- What are your favourite 'war stories' – providing lessons that we might share with our prospective audience – about 'herding cats'?

- What, in your opinion, brings out the best (and worst) in your people?

We – and of course our publishers! – were delighted at the many exceedingly complimentary comments and reviews we received about the modest volume that resulted from these deliberations.

Now, a decade on from the publication of our first edition, much has changed in our world – but a good number of what might be called fundamentals in the 'business' of leading and managing academics and researchers have, in our view, remained constant.

So in preparing this, in essence, '10th Anniversary Edition', reflection and refreshment was of real importance, as has been calibration and additional input from some of our original group of devoted 'consultees', listed as follows, as well as invaluable inputs from some other experienced leaders, who have joined us since the first edition.

We hope we hit the spot with both new and 'old' readers alike.

Acknowledgements

There is an old Chinese saying: 'An evening across the table with a wise man is worth a month of study in books.' We have had the good fortune of many such interactions over the years – perhaps not always a full evening (or even a dinner), but quality time in conversation with wise and informed men and women. Their ideas and experiences have helped forge our own thinking, and are greatly appreciated.

We hope our distillation of their thoughts, and our own, will merit your study.

We are especially indebted to the following people for helping us in our original quest(s) and in this follow-up venture. Their various contributions, non-attributed, appear (in indented italics) throughout our text.

Joan Adams – formerly Vice President, Battelle, USA

Rich Adams – formerly Senior Vice President, Battelle, USA

Stephen Akers – Independent Consultant, Materials Science and Manufacturing, Mollis, Switzerland

Karin Alexander – Independent Consultant, Political Economy Analysis, Cape Town, RSA

Bridget Allchin – formerly of Wolfson College, Cambridge, UK

Sheridan Ash – Director, PricewaterhouseCoopers LLP, UK

Melanie Bagg – CEO, National Youth Science Forum, Australia

Bai Chunli – President of the Alliance of International Science Organisations, and formerly President, Chinese Academy of Sciences, Beijing, China,

Michael Barber – formerly Vice-Chancellor, Flinders University, Australia

Michael Battaglia – Research Director: Sustainability, Agriculture and Food, and Director of FutureFeed, CSIRO, Australia

Robin Batterham – Kernot Professor of Engineering, Melbourne University; formerly Chief Technologist of Rio Tinto and Chief Scientist of Australia

Emma Beckett – NHMRC Career Fellow and Lecturer, School of Environmental & Life Sciences, University of Newcastle, Australia

Genevieve Bell – Distinguished Professor and Director of the 3A Institute, Australian National University

Attila Brungs – Vice-Chancellor, University of Technology Sydney, Australia

Curtis Carlson – Founder and CEO, Practice of Innovation LLC; formerly Chief Executive, SRI International, Menlo Park, USA

Geraldine Chin Moody – Director and Co-Founder, 5H Values Capital, Australia, and formerly Chief Operating Officer, Baker & McKenzie, Australia

Ian Chubb – formerly Chief Scientist, Government of Australia and Vice-Chancellor, Australian National University

Geoffrey Crossick – formerly Warden, Goldsmiths, University of London, and Vice-Chancellor, University of London, UK

Simon Davies – Firmwide Managing Partner, Linklaters LLP

Glyn Davis – Distinguished Professor, Crawford School of Public Policy, Australian National University, and formerly Vice-Chancellor, University of Melbourne, Australia

Ian Dean – International leadership coach, Stellenbosch, RSA

Mark Dodgson – Emeritus Professor, and formerly Director, Technology and Innovation Management Centre, School of Business, University of Queensland, Australia

Annie Duncan – formerly Chair of the Australian Communities Foundation; formerly Chief Executive, Questacon, Australia

Peter Duncan – formerly Chairman, Orica Ltd, and Chief Executive, Shell Australia

David Eastwood – Vice-Chancellor, Birmingham University, UK

Andrew Einhorn – Founder and former CEO, Numeric NPC, Cape Town, RSA

Charles Elachi – formerly Director, Jet Propulsion Lab, USA

Alan Finkel – formerly Chief Scientist, Government of Australia and Chancellor, Monash University, Australia

Boel Flodgren – formerly Professor of Law, and former President of Lund University, Sweden

Ian Frazer – Professor, University of Queensland, and founding CEO of the Translational Research Institute and former Australian of the Year

Margaret Gardner – President and Vice-Chancellor, Monash University, Australia

Julia Goodfellow – formerly Vice-Chancellor, University of Kent, UK, Chair of the British Science Association and President of Universities UK

Geoffrey Green – formerly Senior Partner, Ashurst LLP, UK

John Greene – Emeritus Associate Professor and Senior Scholar, University of Cape Town, RSA

Paul Greenfield – formerly Vice-Chancellor, University of Queensland, Australia

Christina Hickey – Senior Manager, Communications, CSL Ltd, Australia

Peter Høj – Vice-Chancellor and President, University of Adelaide, Australia

Graham Humphries – Fellow, Cox Architecture, Canberra, Australia

Mark Kendall – Vice-Chancellor's Entrepreneurial Professor, Australian Natl. University; Founder/CEO, WearOptimo Pty (Ltd)

Richard Larkins – formerly Chancellor of La Trobe University and Vice-Chancellor, Monash University, Australia

Debbie Lawrence – Group Head, Data Management & Strategy, London Stock Exchange Group, London, UK

Erkki Leppavuori – President of the European Association of Research and Technology Organisations (EARTO), formerly President and CEO VTT Technical Research Centre, Finland

Keith McNeil – Deputy Director General, Department of Health, Queensland, Australia, formerly Chief Executive, Cambridge University Hospitals NHS Foundation Trust, UK

Ramesh Mashelkar – National Research Professor, formerly President, Global Research Alliance and Director General, CSIR National Laboratories, India

Clive Mattieson – formerly Editor, *The Australian,* Sydney, Australia

Graham Mitchell – Chief Executive, Foursight Associates, Melbourne, Australia

David Morley – Senior Partner, Allen & Overy LLP, UK

Robert Morris – Professor, National University of Singapore; formerly VP, Global Labs, IBM Research, Shanghai, China

Tanya Monro – Australian Chief Defence Scientist, and formerly Deputy Vice-Chancellor, Univ. of South Australia

Gus Nossal – formerly Director, Walter and Eliza Hall Institute, Australia; President of the Australian Academy of Science and of the Intl. Union of Immunological Societies

Jim Peacock – CSIRO; formerly Chief Scientist, Government of Australia

David Penington – formerly Vice-Chancellor, University of Melbourne, Australia; and former Chairman of Cochlear Ltd and of Bionic Vision Australia

Ian Powell – formerly Senior Partner, PriceWaterhouse Coopers LLP, UK

Max Price – formerly Vice-Chancellor, University of Cape Town, RSA

Susie Robinson – Executive Director, Australian Plant Phenomics Facility, University of Adelaide, Australia

Alan Robson – Emeritus Professor, Faculty of Science, University of Western Australia, formerly Vice-Chancellor, University of Western Australia

Craig Roy – Chairman of the Board, Silex Systems Ltd, Australia and formerly Deputy Chief Executive, CSIRO, Australia

Louise Ryan – Professor, University of Technology Sydney; formerly Chief, Mathematical and Information Sciences, CSIRO, Australia, and Professor of Biostatistics, Harvard University, USA

Ron Sandland – Chair, Australian Plant Phenomics Facility, University of Adelaide, Australia, formerly Deputy Chief Executive, CSIRO, Australia

Richard Sexton – Executive Board member, PriceWaterhouseCoopers LLP, UK

Bernard Shapiro – formerly Principal, McGill University, Canada

Vince Sharma – Senior Partner, Mills Oakley Pty Ltd, Canberra, Australia

Margaret Sheil – Vice-Chancellor, Queensland University of Technology; formerly Chief Executive, Australian Research Council, Australia

Peter Shergold – Chancellor, Western Sydney University; formerly Head of the Australian Public Service

Fiona Simpson, MP – formerly Speaker of the Queensland Parliament, Brisbane, Australia

Adrian Smith – formerly Vice-Chancellor, University of London; formerly Director General for Science and Research, Department for Business, Innovation and Skills, UK

George Smith – Emeritus Professor of Materials Science, University of Oxford, UK

Mark Stafford-Smith – formerly CEO, Desert Knowledge Cooperative Research Centre, Australia

Ian Steadman – formerly Dean of Arts, Univ. of the Witwatersrand, RSA; formerly Director of Development at the Open University and at Oxford Brookes University, UK

John Stuckey – Senior Partner Emeritus, McKinsey & Company, Australia

Mandy Thomas – formerly Executive Dean, Creative Industries Faculty, Queensland University of Technology, Australia

Rick Trainor – Rector, Exeter College, Oxford, and formerly Principal, King's College London, UK

Jeff Wadsworth – formerly President and CEO, Battelle, USA

David Watson – formerly Master, Green Templeton College, Oxford; formerly Vice-Chancellor, University of Brighton, UK

Paul Wellings – Vice-Chancellor, University of Wollongong, Australia; formerly Vice-Chancellor, Univ. of Lancaster, UK

Bert Westwood – formerly Corporate Vice President of Research and Technology, Lockheed Martin Corporation, USA

David Williams – formerly Dean, College of Engineering, Ohio State University; formerly President, University of Alabama in Huntsville, USA

John Wood – formerly Secretary-General, Association of Commonwealth Universities, London; formerly Chief Executive of the Central Laboratories of the Research Councils, UK

Alex Zelinsky – Vice-Chancellor, University of Newcastle, Australia; formerly Australian Chief Defence Scientist

* * * * *

We are particularly indebted on this occasion to the splendid help from Ian Steadman and – again! – Mark Dodgson and Sheridan Ash; and to Melanie Bagg for her contributions around social media. And, for our previous two books, to Karin Alexander, Geoffrey Green, Ian Dean, David Williams and John Wood; we are most grateful to all these special individuals who generously gave of their time, not only to share their insights, but also as 'key readers' of the two manuscripts, offering numerous helpful suggestions.

Two texts, in particular, provided us with our original inspiration – in very different ways, indeed 'chalk and cheese' some might say: Francis Cornford's *Microcosmographia Academica*, which first appeared in 1908, and from which we have borrowed the sentiment for our sub-title; and Robert Townsend's *Up the Organization* (1970) which provided a helpful, alphabetical 'taxonomy' for arranging the substantial feedback we received. These two volumes, written six decades apart, are also direct and to the point, a practice which we have tried to follow in our own text.

We are also grateful to Sean Davies of Amrop Cordiner King, Melbourne for supplying copies of their excellent career booklets, *Taking Charge* and *Maintaining the Balance*, which provided us with a guide to the useful consultation and quotation approach we have employed, we hope with positive effect.

Special thanks are again due to Biddy Greene of Cape Town for editorial support – without her eagle-eyed professionalism and her cheerful, constructive input we would have had a much less polished manuscript. Also, to all of the team at our publishers, Triarchy Press, under their Editor, Andrew Carey, for their enthusiasm, advice and commitment.

We would once again like to acknowledge, with thanks, the encouragement and learning opportunities provided, over many years, by our respective institutions, and by our splendid colleagues therein.

Finally, we wish you well in your own 'cat-herding' adventures and would be very pleased to hear about your own experiences.

Geoff Garrett
Graeme Davies

Canberra & Newark-on-Trent ~ December 2020

geoff.g.garrett@gmail.com
graeme.davies@london.ac.uk

How to use this book

Read it.

In any order.

Maybe with a pencil/pen/highlighter in your hand – which you
should USE.

If you thought it was helpful, read it again in six months' time.

Perhaps with a different-coloured pencil/pen/highlighter!

And if you just want to dip in, then the CONTENTS list and
INDEX will help.

How the book works

As you might have skipped the Foreword, Introduction and so on, here, before you begin, is a labelled example to show you how we've constructed this book:

Academics and researchers would usually prefer life to contain no 'administrators' whatsoever. Except perhaps in the libraries, and of course on payday.

> *When I worked at the university there was a huge divide between academics and administrators. Any academic who was 'promoted' to the administrative section was seen as a 'sell-out'.*

> "Leadership is the art of getting someone else to do something you want done because he wants to do it." Dwight D. Eisenhower (1890-1969)

So, what does this mean in terms of the management–leadership dimension? How best to cope with these often brilliant and often recalcitrant individuals? – and certainly they (you?) see themselves as very individual!

This is the main text – by us, the authors.

The bits in indented italics are words of wisdom gleaned from our colleagues and friends. They show you that YOU ARE NOT ALONE!

Words indented and in quotes are quotations from 'famous people' that we couldn't resist adding.

Us again. Telling you what we think…

* * * * *

Each of the four parts (Chapters A to D) – which package the 'key topics' of our twelve sections – commences with some introductory scene-setting, and concludes with an executive summary labelled 'In Conclusion'.

At the end of the book, our Postscript attempts to encapsulate, in a page or so, the essence of what we address in the text.

Introduction

Academic and research institutions have one critically important characteristic in common when it comes to considering how they might best be led and managed. Both are staffed by women and men of high intellectual ability who pride themselves on their skill at thinking and acting creatively, and independently. There is usually no culture of uniformity. 'Command and control' approaches rarely prosper; time scales, to get things done, may be lengthy, if not sometimes glacial; disagreement, ubiquitous.

This means that the staff of academic institutions (universities and colleges) and the staff of research institutions (government research organisations and research councils) as well as the research groups of many commercial companies and government departments, can require a set of leadership and management skills somewhat different from (but of course with many parallels to) those often considered more characteristic of the world of commerce, industry and finance. The 'carrot' will certainly predominate over the 'stick', and the carrots will vary.

There is a place for guile and political acumen. It is this that leads to the metaphor of 'herding cats' – if you have to try to coordinate a very difficult situation, where people want to do very different things, you're herding cats.

Our aim in this slim volume is to show that the trick with 'cats' (and by that we mean with many academics and researchers) is to know that it is a lot harder to push them to a destination than it is to tempt them to an outcome.

That is, of course, what makes managing them so challenging. And so rewarding.

* * *

In bringing together our thoughts and the thoughts of others, we have sought, in the way we have organised the material, to follow the sort of timeline that a new leader and manager faces on taking office or a more experienced leader in moving 'up' or 'across' to a new set of challenges and opportunities.

Of course, these do not form a simple sequence since there will necessarily be much overlap. We believe that good leaders and managers must be able to deal with these matters both in parallel and in succession.

Thus there is, first, the need to understand the cultural climate in which the new leader's (often multiple) roles are carried out. This cultural climate comprises not only the culture of the department, or institution, but also aspects of the broader social, political and ideological terrain. Then, attention must be given to mastering the priorities of getting on with the new role(s).

As one's skills and experience build, the need to be on top of the people-management issues becomes paramount. Lastly, for the longer term, formulating strategy and implementing change take precedence.

* * *

Finally, in addition to the obvious (and somewhat fortuitous, and only marginally forced) Cat linkages – the 'twelve Cs' of our Contents emerged from our jointly seeking to identify, and summarise for ourselves, key learnings from our own deliberations and consultations. They merely provide advice and are certainly not 'Commandments'!

We trust that they will provide a useful aide-memoire for those in academia and research aspiring to be leaders, or to be better leaders.

A: UNDERSTANDING THE CULTURE

'Culture' has, so conventional wisdom goes, a significant influence on all dimensions of organisational life; it is often described as 'the way we do things around here'.

While there are obvious differences between academic and research institutions and groups – largely associated with differing missions and outcomes – the cultural dimensions of both are notoriously complex.

In seeking to provide guidance to aspiring (and practising) leaders in this environment, we have chosen, in the sections that follow, to address cultural issues that we – and, we would say, the majority of the colleagues we consulted – believe are ripe, and indeed a priority, for reflection. And, a decade on from the first edition of this book, they remain so.

These include:

- the relatively conservative nature of the culture forged, and still often influenced, by history

- the high IQ of the workforce

- their correspondingly high ideals but commonly challenging style

- the often bureaucratic nature of many institutional processes and 'administrations'

- the immense difficulties, and huge advantages, in seeking cross-boundary collaboration

- the nature of conflict – political, emotional, historical – and suggestions for its effective resolution (or at least understanding) in a 'cats' environment.

1. Aspects of the CULTURE

In the Introduction we made the point that academic and research institutions have a culture all of their own. Accepting this, and then gaining an understanding of that culture, is critical to leading and managing in these institutions.

There are significant differences of culture in the wide range of activities embraced within the 'business' of academic and research management. These cannot all be reconciled, so it is necessary to reinforce the conviction that being part of the bigger team is the thing you have in common.

We first consider some background issues, central to developing an understanding of culture in the academic/ research environment. We then go on to explore a range of other issues, many of which embrace concepts involving change. In our concluding section (Section 12), we return to address further issues and approaches for leading sustainable change.

Cats will not be commanded... This fact – that cats are generally unwilling to be instructed – requires the cat-herder's understanding of just what it is that leadership demands in this environment.

> *Academics like to lead but they do not like being led. I often felt more like a gardener – watering a little here, weeding a little there, trying to cross-fertilise or simply trying to make things grow where the long shadows from the giant trees (professors) made it difficult for anything to grow.*

> *You cannot, in our sort of organisation, order people about.*

You can, of course, but it won't get you very far, even in the short term.

> *Academics do not respond well to managerialism or rules or instructions.*

One of my colleagues was senior in the Army before he joined our ranks. He remarked, "In the Army we used to argue like mad, but when the decision was made, that was it. A hundred per cent alignment, and a focus on action, and getting the job done. In this place, when the decision is made it seems to signal the starting gun for the debate to commence in earnest, using all the 'political' weapons at people's disposal!"

Coming from industry, I found the culture in this specialist research organisation so very different... primarily around the need for scientific autonomy and with success measured by individual credibility and individual performance... 'top-down' doesn't work in our type of organisation.

There is a real difference when you're having to get everything done through influence as opposed to through authority.

Learning from history...

"Those who cannot remember the past are condemned to repeat it." George Santayana (1863-1952)

In most institutions, for better or for worse, the culture at any particular time is frequently determined by the immediate past, as well as being influenced, to a greater or lesser extent, by the more distant past. Thus...

Clear thinking about the history, nature and direction, and development of your particular institution or group... is imperative. The past lives on in most institutions, influencing attitudes and judgements in a manner which is often deeply hidden. Successfully managing change depends on getting these issues out into the open.

This recognition of the influence of the past may explain to some extent the view that...

Universities are inherently conservative institutions because of their wide diversity of cultures.

5

An old university... has a very special culture, nourished by a strong self-esteem and a feeling of being a very important institution in society, but, at the same time, it has a very inward-looking culture. The long history – which is something that really counts in the university world – adds to the prestige... (and) makes it difficult for the leader to try to 'modernise' the institution in different ways.

Historically, different disciplines have developed some quite different cultures – the same thinking and approach usually doesn't work across the board.

And 'bagging' the past, rather than building on, and from it, may not be the best way to go... I think it's really important to celebrate what has been accomplished and not knock it. To resist the temptation to go negative about other people's decisions and put them down in seeking to pull yourself up.

So understanding the cultural 'landscape', and its history, may help clarify a considerable range of situations and decisions, and make them more comprehensible. And help craft your future strategy:

"The further backward you can look, the further forward you can see." Winston Churchill (1874-1965)

Why are we here?... Academics and researchers are clever people, and clever people normally function in ways quite different from others. They can revel in – indeed even exploit – the complex. Thus, in stark contrast to the old adage about genius being the art of making the complex seem simple...

Many experts want to wrap their subject up and make it seem very difficult, and far beyond a normal person's understanding, thus showing that they're very clever. It can be all about preserving a mystique.

They can also revel in the minutiae...

6

It's amazing how so many very clever people just focus on the detail and then only on the detail that applies to them. And frequently very trivial detail at that.

Nevertheless, it is important to recognise that…

Mostly our people are motivated to help shape how, through their teaching, the next generation see the world; or how, through their research, they can actually change the world.

In addition, certain core values are intrinsic and ubiquitous – most particularly, the pursuit of excellence and including the recognition of the importance of fairness and equity.

The political bias…

I wish I had known earlier that I needed to think more politically and not only down the 'straight and narrow' scientific path.

Notwithstanding the need to be persuasive, it is essential to recognise that this may also require appeals (of varying strength) to prejudice and to political motivations…

"The Political Motive in the academic breast is honest enough. It is Fear -- genuine, perpetual, heartfelt timorousness… The proper objects of Fear are, in order of importance: giving yourself away; females (sic); what Dr ---- will say; the public washing of [dirty] linen…This is the central mystery of academic politics." Francis Cornford (1874-1943)

Talking straight… This can be a real dilemma. Being open, transparent and honest will inevitably imply communicating some bad news. Correctly managed, straight talk can establish the 'burning platform' motivation for change. Badly handled, it can provide a *cause célèbre* and an opportunity for your opponents to use every available channel (mainstream media, social media, politicians, government bureaucrats, your staff) to communicate that, actually, it is you who are the problem.

When I arrived I assumed I could speak straight, and tell them how I saw it. And I did. I soon learned, regrettably, that I had to speak more like a politician – congratulate the questioner on his intelligent observations; not answer the question directly; answer the question with a question; etc. It is a sadness. If I disagreed with people it was not an academic argument, I was being authoritative.

But at times this may not be wholly appropriate:

If you've got bad news, you'd better front up. Pretending is a bad idea.

Honesty is always respected, even if it causes a stir – sometimes it's good to create a stir – that is, not always to be a 'politician'.

So, while we feel that straightness has definite virtues, all good leaders will need to develop the ability to judge how and when these differing approaches need to be balanced.

Bureaucracy rules, OK?… It can be convenient to blame many problems and issues on the bureaucratic nature of the institution. However…

The biggest thing that I have found out through the years is people in research are actually bureaucrats. I would have expected them all to be interested in the future, wanting to change the world, brimming over with enthusiasm to get on with the job and deliver useful results. This took me a long time to realise and I think I would have been much more effective if I had understood that there are a lot of people who really do not want to see much in the way of change, and that includes a lot of people in R&D.

Consider this sentiment within the definition (from Chambers Dictionary): **bureaucracy** (*noun*)… any system of administration in which matters are hindered by excessive adherence to minor rules and procedures.

And we know that, left unattended, bureaucracies can tend to bloat, recognising that – as Cyril Northcote Parkinson (of

Parkinson's Law fame) observed:

> "There need be little or no relationship between the work to be done and the size of the staff to which it may be assigned."

Noting also…

> "Rational bureaucrats… will always and everywhere seek to increase their budgets in order to increase their own power." William A. Niskanen (1933-2011) US economist and Chairman of the Cato Institute.

For these reasons, bureaucracy can be anathema to many, if not all, of our academic and research colleagues. Nevertheless, we recognise that there is inherent bureaucracy in academic and research institutions as encapsulated in the view that…

> *Universities are extraordinarily rules-based institutions.*

This perspective does not seem to have changed much over the last hundred years:

> "(One) must never be troubled with having to think whether this or that ought to be done or not; it should be settled by rules. Plainly, the more rules you can invent, the less need there will be to waste time over fruitless puzzling about right and wrong. The best sort of rules are those which prohibit important, but perfectly innocent, actions, such as smoking in College courts, or walking to Madingley on Sunday without academical dress." Francis Cornford (1874-1943)

The trouble with this, of course, is that…

> *Unnecessary, unexplained red tape is a killer of morale.*

Most particularly, in a difficult financial environment, bureaucracy can flourish.

> *When the budgets got tough, the bureaucrats got into high gear: a junior colleague remarked "Sometimes it feels like we have difficulty in getting a chair moved around here!".*

Vigilance is needed – in good financial times as well as bad – for excessive red tape to be avoided. This can pay real motivational dividends:

The active minimisation of unnecessary red tape and good explanations around why some bureaucratic processes are necessary, if they cannot be avoided, scores high 'brownie points' in the motivation business.

Good research leaders give a sense of being 'on the side' of the researcher (and of common sense), seeking a way around bureaucratic obstacles rather than hiding behind them.

And there is light at the end of the tunnel…

Academics will be persuaded by reason and, by and large, are driven by the same altruistic intent that has driven them to a life in academia. Thus, if the guiding principles are 'to achieve excellence in education and research' and the argument can be made that – given the prevailing constraints, for example the need for financial responsibility and viability, efficient management to avoid chaos, accountability to meet the requirements of government, students and the general community, etc. – if all your actions and those you are wishing your staff to pursue are in the ultimate interests of excellence in education and research, then by and large the academic staff will seek to do what you would like them to do.

2. On CONFLICT

"Most academic persons, when they carry on studying – not only in youth as part of their education, but as the prime pursuit of their maturer years – become decidedly queer." Plato (429-347 BC)

'Cats' come with extraordinary talent and abilities; but on the counter side, they often come with major issues and you get left picking up the pieces.

Funny places… By their very nature, academic and research institutions can be rather strange environments. They can be worlds of their own and not at all like 'normal' workplaces. This reflects both the characteristics of the staff and the nature of their pursuits.

Universities and the like are peculiar places – they are professionally questioning and argumentative communities – more or less everybody is authorised to have an opinion about everything. And issues tend to generate heat in inverse proportion to their importance.

This can manifest itself in conflicts of varying degrees of intensity. Conflict may be hard, at first, to identify. For example:

The first thing a committee member might say may well be the exact opposite of what he or she means. "I'd like to agree with everything the Chairman has just said, but…" or "With respect…" (often meaning quite the opposite).

It is also extraordinary how myopic and bloody-minded some very intelligent people can be when issues are outside their comfort zone, or (especially) when issues potentially affect their comfort zone in an adverse way.

In many situations, whatever your or the collective decision, you will always upset one group or another. Even doing nothing will upset some people.

> *No decision you ever make will receive universal support. Abolishing the difference in car parking between the academic and the professional support staff led to the greatest criticism of any decision I made.*

Thus, people who in their 'normal' professional lives generate and interrogate evidence and draw (mostly) sensible conclusions, become suspicious, spurn a logical argument out of hand or provide forty-seven – often mostly spurious – reasons why 'it' can't, or shouldn't, be done: "There's no way I can move offices in July; I have exams to mark."

Peer pressure… In seeking to resolve conflict, sensible peer pressure, carefully harnessed, can be helpful and facilitate the effective management of change:

> *If the well-respected Mary or Fred down the corridor says "That's a good idea", hitherto illogically-argued resistance around 'issues of principle' may suddenly fall away.*

Techniques for dealing with opposition, and resistance… You will perhaps have noticed by now that Francis Cornford's name crops up regularly. Cornford (1874-1943) was an English classical scholar and poet, and a Fellow of Trinity College, Cambridge. His excellent little book *Microcosmographia Academica*, subtitled *Being a Guide for the Young Academic Politician*, written just over a century ago, focuses on the political realities and intrigues of academic life and, as we mentioned in our acknowledgements, we have found it remarkably pertinent to our current endeavour. For leaders/managers in academia and research we believe it could usefully be required reading. Many of Cornford's observations remain as alive and well today as they were more than a hundred years ago:

> "The Principle of the Dangerous Precedent is that you should not now do an admittedly right action for fear you, or your equally timid successors, should not have the courage to do right in some future case."

"The Fair Trial Argument – 'give the present system a fair trial'...is especially useful in withstanding changes."

"The Alternative Proposal [is] an accepted means of obstruction... As soon as three or more alternatives are in the field, there is pretty sure to be a majority against any one of them, and nothing will be done."

"The Last Ditch [is] a place which you may safely threaten to die in... if you did die, nobody would much mind; but the threat may frighten them for the moment."

"Wasting Time is another method of obstruction... the simplest method [here] is [to be] Boring. Talk slowly and indistinctly, at a little distance from the point. While you are engaged in [being] Boring it does not matter much what you talk about; but, if possible, you should discourse upon the proper way of doing something which you are notorious for doing badly for yourself. Thus, if you are an inefficient lecturer, you should lay down the law on how to lecture.... You should make six words do duty for one... and fill up the time – until you can think of something to say – by talking."

On clarity... Later in this book (Sections 4 and 9) we talk more about the importance of being clear about where we're headed (goals) and "who must do what by when" (roles and responsibilities), and about communicating these clearly. When this doesn't happen, conflict is nigh:

Most of the strife I've observed (and no doubt contributed to) in organisations I have worked in has arisen from us not being clear about what we need to get done, and who's responsible for what.

No popularity contest... The existence of conflict makes it very clear that being at the head of an organisation or group is not easy. Nor is it necessarily a reflection of universal admiration and approval!

With conflict comes unpopularity. The decision maker may often be criticised more than the decision, particularly where there is perceived disadvantage to an individual or a group:

"A man who dies without enemies is a man who has changed nothing and most probably contributed little in his lifetime." Walter Murdoch (1874-1970) Australian academic and essayist.

Once you have made decisions and are acting on these, don't worry that people will criticise you or try to undermine you. Don't take this personally or be offended – accept this is as part of the change process.

Noting that, personally, this can be very uncomfortable:

If you're a human being you don't like to be disliked, and especially not hated. I'm a human being too.

The hardest thing I learned is that you can't, ever, keep everyone happy. It was a problem for me, as I like being liked.

It can be very difficult to get people to support you. Be prepared to get all sorts of negative feedback. It will be nasty. It was very difficult for me.

Be careful in looking at what is written about yourself. Whether it's from the student newspaper, your local media or on Twitter or Facebook. You don't need to read all the 'bad news'. Control the inflow of stuff that keeps you awake at night.

But on the plus side, our experience is that most dark clouds have silver linings:

Conflict situations can often provide a good opportunity to turn negative thinking into positive strategies.

The power that I do have is to call people to the table. People with nominally polarised views. I give them a space where they can talk with some safety. We put aside stuff we can't agree on and focus on the things that we can do something about and reach a solution.

Sterling advice.

And remember... of the handful of Golden Rules, one most certainly is: "Where there is conflict in life, there are always two sides to every story".

3. The difficulty of COLLABORATION and boundary crossing

"How easily men could make things better than they are – if only they tried together." Winston Churchill (1874-1965)

Most of the smart people around are not in your own organisation.

Holding hands in the traffic… Many lessons about life have been instilled in us from an early age. Robert Fulghum's thought-provoking and pithy best-seller *All I Really Need to Know I Learned in Kindergarten* (1988) records that these wisdoms – for nations as well as for individuals and organisations – were found "not at the top of the graduate school mountain, but there in the sandpit at pre-school". Thus, we are expected to "play fair… clean up your own mess… say sorry when you hurt somebody" – and lots more.

Fulghum also takes us back to when we were five or six years old, and our teacher led us on an exciting outing, to the fire station or the chocolate factory: "When you go out into the world, watch out for traffic, hold hands, and stick together." Never truer words. There's a lot of heavy traffic out there, in our world.

We still, and continually, need to be asking our front-line researchers, at all levels: 'Who are you holding hands with? Who are the best of the best in your line? When did you last interact with them? When are they coming to visit?'

So it's all about team stuff: T.E.A.M. – 'Together Everyone Achieves More', as the old saying goes. We are, after all…

"…each of us angels with only one wing; and we can only fly by embracing one another." Luciano de Crescenzo (1928-2019) Italian writer, film actor, director and engineer.

Collaboration is not the easy option… Unfortunately the prevailing culture is, by and large, not supportive of extensive collaboration. There appears to be a form of generic resistance…

Academics etc. can be profoundly bad at collaboration. All the performance drivers are geared towards individual attainment.

One of the things I do most is trying to persuade people to put aside self-interest to achieve a better outcome.

I hear strong, and successful collaborators harshly criticised with 'How do we know they are good in their own right if they've done all their work with others?'

It's really hard getting people to understand why collaboration is so important and that these are higher-order skills they need to acquire. They can acknowledge this intellectually, but every fibre in their body (and their experience, and history) is pointing diametrically in the other direction.

It may, of course, be that those who would be affected have no experience (or only limited experience) of collaborating in meaningful ways. As a consequence the leader often has to go out on a limb proactively to push through in this arena.

We continually underestimate the tendency and ability of individuals and groups to silo themselves. And we still have to work very hard to get communication across groups that we thought were communicating.

Particularly important in research organisations is the need to operate with what Jack Welch, when CEO at General Electric, called 'boundarylessness' – the need is exceeded only by the difficulty in doing so.

Over a two-year period I had to pull together a bunch of institutionally independent players, forge a coalition and hold it together long enough to build a structure and get focus. It was the hardest thing I ever had to do. I walked away exhausted.

The System – help or hindrance?... It is also far from clear whether or not the systems in which academics and researchers operate are intrinsically helpful or, conversely, provide some form of inherent obstacles:

The world has become so much more complex, with so much more access to information. So much is happening and so many ideas are generated across the 'horizontal', yet we're still dealing with management systems that operate, and get fed, from the vertical.

So much in the system works against collaboration: the departmental setting, the subjects' own tradition, the financing system, the researchers and teachers themselves, everything. It's a miracle when multidisciplinary initiatives succeed!

By and large, people work together well because of personal chemistry and cohesion of interests rather than because they are directed to do so. However, structure and management can facilitate and enable more such interactions or – more often – can impede them.

Today's successful innovation is 'multi-everything' – culture, institution, nation, product, market. People who are (going to be) successful in our world can operate across systems, languages, governments – we don't teach this in our universities. It's mostly still all about extremely 'deep but narrow'.

But enhancing collaboration is an arena where access to resources can be a very powerful driver. Funding can be used both to support the initiation of collaboration and to promote its maintenance, and even to encourage intellectual jumps that cross previously obstructive boundaries:

Money is about the only real driver I've got to encourage collaboration. So I say, "If you want to run a sole operation, get your own money. If you want strong and tangible institutional support, you've got to show us who you are seriously collaborating with."

You also do need to be careful how you use labels. The answer to the (rhetorical) "What's in a name?" question is, actually, "Quite a lot"…

They (upper management) were preaching long and hard about the importance of us all working collaboratively across institutional boundaries. Yet they've organised us in 'Divisions' … interesting mixed messages there!

Collaboration can create real benefits… Collaboration may not be easy; it may be resisted; it may face inherent system-based difficulties, but in the long run it can provide vitality and creativity.

"The most important knowledge is not inside the boundaries of an organisation. You don't achieve it through containerization, you achieve it through collaboration." Don Tapscott (1947-) Canadian business executive, author and consultant.

Here, sometimes we confuse cause and effect. In other words, is collaboration causative of, or associated with, good outcomes? And again I think there's a false dichotomy between competition and collaboration. Often we need a bit of both.

Boundaries emerge when colleagues build 'Chinese walls' around their areas of responsibility and/or expertise, inhibiting information flow and shared understanding. These boundaries are not just those between operational areas within the organisation; increasingly, they also embrace the boundaries between services and other activities outside the organisation. Internal collaboration important in itself, but it can also send strong messages to those outside about the organisation's ability to encourage *external* collaboration. Boundaries need to be made transparent and permeable to ideas and influences. This can be a very enriching process, both for individuals and for the organisation:

Most exciting innovation happens at those strange interfaces between disciplines.

Don't hesitate to send your best fundamental scientists out to visit production plants, working in areas about which they know nothing (usually over their strong objections). Often they see things that those closer to the operations have missed, and in my organisation's case, this approach led to major developments in the smelting of aluminium, blasting technology and the optimisation of dyeing processes.

It's amazing the stuff you stumble across working outside your own discipline.

My watershed experience about innovation? A good many years back, while responsible for a big mining research division (in South Africa), yearly deaths underground from rock bursts and rock falls in gold mining exceeded 300. Despite major investments and a large, quality research group, impact was minimal. Lab experiments and nice journal papers just weren't cutting it. Until we sent researchers (reluctantly!) underground for an extended period, working cheek by jowl, as they say, with on-site mining engineers and shift bosses – and to great effect. So what happened? 1: Long-lasting personal relationships with key customers/stakeholders were built. 2: 'Technology travels on 2 legs' – or, putting it another way, 'tech transfer is a contact sport' – sound, hard-won insights from the researchers got taken up in real time. And 3: The researchers re-set their research agenda for the next three years as they properly understood the nature of the priority problems, first hand. The moral of the story? Innovation is 'ideas successfully applied', and mobility is key. Don't just sit around your office/research lab if you are wanting to make a real impact 'out there'.

It is encouraging to reflect that the future of 'the boundaries' in our science business are at risk. We firmly believe that most future value-adding innovation will emerge from activities that lie in the gaps between disciplines:

"The twenty-first century, unlike the previous ones, will be typified by synergy, the cross-fertilization between all three fields [the quantum revolution, the computer revolution and the biomolecular revolution], which will mark a sharp turning point in the development of science. The cross-pollination between these three revolutions will be vastly accelerated and will enrich the development of science, giving us unprecedented power to manipulate matter, life and intelligence. In fact, it will be difficult to be a research scientist in the future without having some working knowledge of all these three areas. Already, scientists who do not have some understanding of these three revolutions are finding themselves at a distinct competitive disadvantage." Michio Kaku (1947-) American theoretical physicist, futurist and science communicator.

Great creativity often emerges from the periphery, whether the periphery is geographical, disciplinary, or cultural.

On commercialisation... As we have just mentioned, "Innovation is 'ideas successfully applied'". So, with 'impact' becoming an increasingly important part of research grant review and institutional evaluation, there is a strong argument for asking the (rhetorical) question: if we do great research, but the fruits of our labours fail to reach the outside world, if they fail to create jobs, wealth or improvement in the quality of our lives, and of this planet's life – shouldn't we try harder? Or perhaps try a different tack?

By the way, on 'impact' – a word that is, sadly, becoming a little hackneyed:

What do I mean by impact? Well, when you're playing billiards or snooker, and your cue ball 'impacts' another ball, it generally results in a change of speed and/or direction, hopefully (though not always!) with a positive result. That's what I mean.

So, 'getting stuff out there to make a difference' often requires

21

close collaboration – and strong relationships – between researchers and industry players, aiming to 'commercialise' an idea or an invention, etc. Much has been written about the challenges of this process, around Intellectual Property negotiations, bridging the 'valley of death', the time it (usually) takes, and the like. But we will restrict our input to what we see as a few of the most important points.

We are not just talking about researcher/industry interactions…

So much great research out of our universities and research institutions gets 'lost in translation'. All too rarely does it get properly imported into, for example, public policy development. Most academics and researchers don't get their hands dirty in this space, whereas they should be up to their elbows in providing evidence to support choices, recognising that, in the public policy world, where politics comes into play, there's rarely one right answer.

To optimise the chance of effective 'commercialisation', you need a supportive culture. However…

Universities are very often highly risk averse and as such they don't like researchers taking risks. You've got to keep fighting to get them to take appropriate risks. It's gradually changing, happily, but often commercialisation is not embedded in the culture, i.e. 'the way we do things around here'.

We should celebrate when someone becomes an inventor. What is needed is a culture that values this… with a light touch and good will to look after the inventor, and back them, then they will look after you. Sadly I had to fight hard in a risk-averse culture. It was exhausting.

Backing up a supportive culture requires some different skills:

Effective commercialisation needs highly professional and experienced skills. Get expert advice as early as you can. Beware 'amateur hour'.

And, finally, here is some important advice – both motivating and sobering – for the individual academic/researcher embarking on this path:

You never forget being awarded your first patent. To be an inventor is an awesome feeling. But 'going commercial' is hard.

You must keep your spirits up. Everything you do is a learning exercise... Like talking to potential investors: learn from it, especially when the first response is a 'no'.

You have to be honest with yourself, and figure out who you want to be. Is going this route your passion? In which case you need to go 'all in'. If it's just ticking a box for your CV, it's probably not going to end well.

On negotiation .... which is part and parcel of the leadership assignment. Whether discussing a new research contract, the need for funding for new facilities or equipment, or replacing a teaching programme, we need to know how to best approach the challenge. Here is a handful of 'guideposts' that may be helpful...

"When it comes to negotiation, we prioritise 6 core principles:

1: Build strong relationships ahead of time. (And during negotiations, understand what your counterpart cares about.)

2: Pay close attention to process.

3: Remember the stakeholders who are not at the table, and keep them informed.

4: Avoid self-imposed deadlines.

5: Behave like a trusted partner – or pay the price.

6: Don't let political pressure get in the way of pragmatic solutions.

And there is usually the opportunity to be creative!"

Paul Fisher, Director of the Oxford Programme on Negotiation and Associate Fellow of the Said Business School, University of Oxford.

All good advice, perhaps with one rider with regard to #4: sometimes setting deadlines – even tight ones – can help you keep focused on an important issue (and not get deflected by all the other stuff in your job jar), and maintain momentum.

Collabronauts – the 'Cats' of the future?... So, despite these difficulties, there are strong signs that the future belongs to the boundary-crosser and skilled collaborator. Rosabeth Moss Kanter of Harvard University has elegantly coined a spacefaring analogy by introducing the concept of 'collabronauts', who are...

> "...good at making connections, both human and intellectual. They are constantly on the look-out for new ways to benefit from combining forces with partners. They venture into unfamiliar territory, make deals, and return with knowledge that transforms their home base. They bring organisations closer together, introduce people and build relationships among groups that can initially seem like aliens to one another. They manage rumours, mount peace-keeping missions and solve problems. They convince their colleagues to forget old rules and try something new, something that comes with having partners."

UNDERSTANDING THE CULTURE – In Conclusion

The culture of the typical 'cats' environment is often replete with remarkable intellects, passion, argument, politics (with a small 'p') and prejudice – mostly based on an inheritance from the different disciplines that have influenced those populating the environment. If these characteristics conflict with your own work-life philosophies, you will probably not be comfortable; indeed you are likely to be frustrated. Accept and embrace these qualities of your cats and you will find your work life remarkably enjoyable.

Cultural development is often closely linked with, and nuanced by, particular aspects of the institutional history. This must be understood – and be seen to be understood – if you are to take a lead in institutional progress. Transformation is far from easy – it can be all-consuming and a long journey – one not to be taken on 'unadvisedly, lightly or wantonly'.

Bureaucracy can predominate, despite its being abhorrent to many practising academics and researchers, themselves often bureaucrats at heart, who can become embroiled in trivia, while – at the same time – being engaged in intellectual pursuits and perhaps seeking to change the world. Tread warily, and with careful forethought, but the successful elimination of inappropriate 'red tape' can win both plaudits and improved institutional efficiency.

The future – of discovery, and delivery-of-benefit – will increasingly be characterised by crossing (some might say transgressing) conventional boundaries and breaking down desperately-defended silos. But this – and multi-party collaborations, large and small – is DIFFICULT. Persist. Evangelise. And gradually (perhaps even by stealth) reshape your institutional systems and measures of individual and organisational performance to reinforce collaborative behaviour and enhance the culture. Seek out and reward early 'movers and shakers'. The benefits in enhanced vitality, creativity and productivity will thrill.

B: GETTING THE JOB DONE

Leadership is all about getting results. You stand or fall by your ability to 'get the job done'. How you do it will be personal.

We often talk about cat herding as a serious 'craft'... by which we mean ingenuity and judgement in melding solutions to problems in the face of imperfect information.

Your book's title and my job description are pretty synonymous – actually, I think the three main headings in the position description are: herd cats, crack safes (through legal means only – strategy and charm) and design successful futures (no crystal ball provided).

There are challenges, of course, common to any leadership assignment, whether it be managing a supermarket, running the fire brigade or being a university dean. We have, therefore, chosen to address a range of issues which include, *inter alia*: setting priorities and managing your time; taking decisions and delegating responsibilities; dealing with failure and understanding yourself; managing performance and handling financial setbacks. And so on.

But the 'cats' environment, in our experience and through our observation, can add an overlay of intrigue and complexity. For example, decision making – however sound, necessary and fact-based – can initiate what amounts to trench warfare. You're dealing with exceptionally intelligent people, many of whom believe they know more than you do about everything (and indeed they may well do, at one level). And with so much time spent – and possibly wasted – in the ubiquitous committee meetings and discussion groups, effective management towards results – which are usually much less tangible than they are in 'business' – can be an art form.

4. Taking CHARGE

Leading and managing begin in earnest on the day that you take up your new duties, either through taking up a new post from outside or by being promoted internally. However, you will almost certainly be thinking about your new role from the day when you are appointed – indeed, probably from well before that, as you prepared for the interview process.

First impressions count... For those moving to a new institution: you will be gaining a great deal of knowledge about that institution and about those who will be your new colleagues. Here – or equally, if you are taking up a new role in your current organisation – as a new leader you have a narrow opportunity window to make a good impression. Especially the first time round. Then you're stuck with the old maxim: "You never get a second chance to make a first impression."

The first days need to be approached with care, taking into account not only the particular knowledge you have gained about the new environment and your new responsibilities, but also the range of skills that you have learned over the years in the various posts that you will have held as you moved up the professional ladder.

> *There are some things that I knew at the start and have just been unchanging: the need to be enthusiastic but reasonable, the need to have a sound grasp of fundamentals and being able to discuss things meaningfully across a range of topics.*

> *Trust your instincts, but be prepared to revisit them in the light of experience.*

In making these first impressions, peer credibility can be important; researchers respect other successful researchers. In contrast...

> *It's hard to lead a charge if you look funny on a horse.*

You've got to have credibility, and their respect, and show that you are on their side, batting for them. Then they'll move mountains for you. Alignment, trust and respect are key to getting anything done.

Out and about…

There's a real danger in sitting in your office, and not moving around much. Getting out there builds relationships; and people 'just telling you stuff' is often very valuable.

Much has been written about 'managing by walking about'. It applies as much to 'herding cats' as it does in business. Thus, the 'leader' who lives primarily in his or her office will usually be seen as remote. This will be reinforced if individuals are 'summoned to the presence'. Of course, when several of the management team are involved, the logical place to get together is in a central office or a conference room. On the other hand, going 'walkabout' to see colleagues in their own offices – ideally physically, but increasingly virtually – can be really advantageous in a variety of ways: it helps you understand their situation, their interests, and perhaps pressures and 'happenings' in their lives. It encourages approachability and, most usefully, it allows easier control of the length of the exchange. It is also beneficial for your colleagues' staff to see you 'out and about'.

In my first week as a new young professor, the Registrar called (himself!) – and from 'on high' (the 11th floor) – to say "Hi, and welcome", and fixed a time to come and see me in my shoebox office. I was surprised and delighted. I joined his fan club that day and would always go out of my way to help him.

Walking about also enables ready contacts with colleagues and staff at all levels, and often provides valuable sources of insight and information…

Speak to people openly across the organisation, from the cleaner to the person fixing your computer, to your colleagues… you can learn a lot about what works and what doesn't work throughout the organisation, from people at all levels, by just listening.

In relation to walking the talk… forget it if you think you can run the show, and change things, from your office, by email or through social media. Your people need to see that you're interested – see you talking to people, and watch what you do.

But this is not always possible, as was evident in the 2020 pandemic. Then electronic aids – FaceTime, Zoom etc. – can be used very effectively to maintain 'face-to-face' contacts.

Reality will be different… While advance preparation will obviously stand you in good stead, not least in any job interview process, too much preparation – perhaps leading to some not-necessarily-valid preconceived ideas – may not be helpful:

I'm not sure I'd have liked to know too much ahead of time. I learned most, and quickly, from the experiences I've had, from the mistakes I've made, from observing others – very carefully, and from being thrown in the deep end.

The second day in the job I realised that I was actually on 'the bridge', and in charge. Despite assiduously preparing for several months, I realised that I knew very little about 'the ship'. The preparation to do something and the reality of actually doing it are different.

Appointment bodies tend to emphasise the positives; especially when they have agreed that 'you are the one' and move into sell mode; the reality will be different. Rarely is there deception, more commonly it is naivety. But you soon find out about the warts you have inherited.

You will need to recognise that what helped make you successful in your previous career won't be the same set of skills needed as you move up. Some of those skills will translate and others will not. Any new role will be a steep learning curve.

It is also important to recognise that your learning time cannot be too prolonged – you must quite quickly become engaged with the core business. And early actions and decisions you take will undoubtedly send important messages:

If possible you need an early incident which makes the critical point around intent evident – in my case this was the decision to close a department which was well known to be unacceptably weak.

On managing your time (and your priorities)... In any new role, heavy demands will be imposed upon you. This makes it imperative that you understand how best to manage your time, and this in turn means that you must be able to prioritise your commitments. This is often an area where there is a need to learn fast.

Better time management is something I wish I had learned when I set out on this research leadership path.

One of the best pieces of advice I ever got, from a very wise and significant leader, was that when you get to start managing/leading bigger stuff, you only need to worry about two things: Look after your health, and look after your time.

All too often the 'apparently urgent' can crowd out the important. There are many different approaches to prioritisation but, to be effective, there must be a place for both the large and the small issues. One such approach, advocated by Stephen Covey, author of *The 7 Habits of Highly Successful People* (1989), is built upon the notion of packing rocks of varying size into a jar. Put the sand (small issues) in first and the 'big rocks' (the important things) won't fit in or get dealt with. Put the big rocks in first and it is quite surprising how the rest can be accommodated!

One of the three signs I have on my desk is a card a kind friend sent during one of my more frenetic phases: 'A year from today, will it matter?' This proved to be an excellent filter for the 'big rocks' versus the rest.

The work-life balance…

We recruit people who are ambitious, want work that will challenge and stretch them, and are willing to go the extra mile. But we know that these positive attributes also make them particularly vulnerable to losing balance in their lives.

Enjoying work makes for a fulfilled life. Variety and challenge draw many people to an academic career and are what can make it so engaging. But the danger is that work can too readily dominate lives. There is always something more that could be done, or done better, given more time, and competitive pressures drive people in that direction. And in the long run – while this might be seen to help convert ambition into success – many will regret these choices and the negative fall-out can be not just personal but impact careers, colleagues and ultimately, the institutions for which they work.

Ten years on in the leadership game and I don't have a very good balance between work and the rest of my life… I have a partner who works long hours and has probably been too patient about our lack of time together.

During and since leaving graduate school, getting impossible amounts of work done became a perverse source of pride and a way to keep testing myself; and not even having my five-year old daughter chase me down the street begging me not to go to work was able to shift my focus.

It is very clear that there are increasing pressures on all practising professionals to try to juggle the conflicting demands of activities in the workplace and those of their private and personal lives. These demands impinge on staff at all levels of organisations, from those seeking to establish themselves in their early professional careers to those with a wealth of experience who are taking leading managerial and strategic roles. The work-life balance is an issue which cannot be side-stepped or 'put on the back burner'. It must be addressed and it is not just a 'once in a while' issue.

> One of the most worrying trends in some academic domains is the perceived need to put in 'face time' – where staff feel like they need to be in the office – to be seen even if they don't have work that needs to be done, or if the work can be done from home. As a leader, it is important to show that flexibility can work both in academia and research facilities and still allow service to be delivered at the highest levels.

Thus, recognising the connections between work and 'life', not just the obvious differences, provides important food-for-thought for both the individual and the leader:

> I don't much like the distinction/separation implied in the 'work-life balance' debate. Work is part of life, and many of us derive a lot of satisfaction and intellectual pleasure from our work world – and, indeed, from the value-adding relationships in our social life. This makes it an important concern for us to reflect on.

> Separating work and family life can be false – especially in this age of widespread and constant communication. It's really not clear where one starts and the other ends. And is that necessarily bad? So do recognise that there is the connection.

"I recall the constant exhaustion of trying to survive on as little as three hours sleep and the sensation of always being one step ahead of disaster. I didn't want to give up sooner in the sense that, in an important job at just 33, I was being looked up to as a role model. I didn't want to be an example to young women that it wasn't possible to have a family and do a high-pressure job. So I worked hard to keep both work and family on the agenda." Gaby Hinsliff (1971-) former political editor of *The Observer*.

Overall, the differing demands must be recognised but it is important that a proper balance be maintained – even though that balance may fluctuate. Professional organisations are now focusing to a significant degree on how people can effectively manage their stress and identify ways in which they can maintain their health and wellbeing while at work. For example, exploring ways in which people can adopt a more flexible approach to their work by experimenting with working from home and with other different work patterns.

We do have some way to go before some of the new approaches to the work-life balance issue are adopted as part of our institution's mainstream culture. But there is a growing acceptance that these issues are not going to disappear.

Again there has been much to learn from the 2020 pandemic when 'working from home' supported by electronic communication was the norm for many months, unveiling a 'new normal' work mode for many people.

Stakeholder management... Academic and research institutions engage with a wide and demanding number of stakeholders, ranging from your immediate colleagues in sister institutions to captains (or maybe lieutenants) of industry through to those in the corridors of Government. All – prioritised – will need to be embraced. Needs must be recognised and strategies for fulfilling those needs must be identified.

In achieving this there is no doubt that a 'one size fits all' response won't work. Solutions must match needs, and this does require gaining a very clear understanding of the many and varying characteristics of the needs involved. Often, understanding this will make it necessary for you to see issues from the point of view of the stakeholder, just as much as from the point of view of your own institution.

Don't underestimate – or neglect – your stakeholders; we are sometimes inclined to assume we know more than they do.

Don't tell your key stakeholders what you want to do, and what you want from them. Listen to what they're interested in, and then make the connections with your objectives. Then you'll have their interest, and support.

Very often Government is a major stakeholder. But you don't do business with Government – only with people. All contact should be an exercise in, and an opportunity for, relationship-building and for establishing mutual respect, mutual value add, and trust. If, additionally, you get to like each other, that can be a real bonus. And, as in most relationships, communication is a key issue both in form and content. This can sometimes demand acts of self-denial. For example, it is wise not to ask for financial support from a Minister or official on the first occasion that you meet.

A very senior politician once said to me, no doubt off the record: "Those darn academics are all the same – just like little birds in a nest, always chirping, with their mouths open, and asking for more!"

But this does not mean that your other, non-government stakeholders are less important. Quite the contrary – balancing competing demands is an important skill that needs to be acquired.

Re-emphasising the point: it is critical to build strong relationships with your external contacts…

Years on, when I was asked to summarise the key to the most-would-say-successful organisational survival and transformation process I had had the privilege of leading, I said it could be distilled into one word: "Relationships, relationships, relationships". (Okay, I never was much good at arithmetic.)

People and your time…

"Time spent with cats is never wasted." Sigmund Freud (1856-1939)

Getting results is about understanding the people around you as much as you can, and helping them get the best out of their efforts.

As a preamble in approaching the academic role, I try to divide the issues which colleagues come to you with into three: Nasty: have to be dealt with immediately. Insoluble: been around a long time, people brighter than you have tried to resolve it (so don't worry if you can't – it's okay to have some insolubles which people gnaw on, as long as they're not corrosive). Then lastly, those where you listen, and say "That's a really good point – go and speak to X, Y, Z and have you thought of A, B, C? And let's speak again next week." Often they don't come back next week. And, sometimes, you might even get a 'thank you' email.

Management/leadership is a full-on people business. Initially you will need to engage with both your immediate colleagues and with staff at many different levels in your organisation.

I spend a lot of time with my people, especially if they are new and recruited from the outside, talking about the culture of our institution: how we do things around here, how we operate and how we make decisions.

When I started running an organisation, although I realised that people issues were important, I still did not realise how much time they would take up.

I wish that someone had sat me down and asked me if I was ready to expend most of my energy on the development and growth of others in the service of the shared vision. I wish that I had been told this rather than discovering it by accident.

And, as mentioned above, there will also be non-specialist contacts/stakeholders requiring your personal time, and this may need you to draw upon quite different approaches from those used inside the institution. Here you cannot assume the levels of knowledge of 'the system' that your academic/research colleagues have. This all takes time and there are no easy shortcuts. However, there are aids to progress – and pitfalls to be avoided.

Thus, whether you are interacting 'outside' or 'inside' your organisation, some common wisdoms apply. For example…

Try to learn people's names.

Building credibility and respect takes ten times longer than losing it.

You don't have to show off and try to prove how clever you are: "I don't understand; this is beyond my capabilities" is better. As is making fun of yourself.

People infer as much from what you don't say as they do from what you actually do say.

Follow up by emailing a 'thank you' note, for their time/advice/suggestions.

Don't be afraid to ask 'stupid' questions since there are no such things. The Scots have a wonderful, 'third-party' approach which is to ask the 'daft laddie' question. Instead of using a self-deprecating approach: "…this may be a stupid question, but why are you doing A not B…?", they frequently adopt the line "…a daft laddie might ask why you're doing A not B…". Once you have found an equivalent phrase that suits you, you will be well set up.

Don't forget your external 'Supporters' Club'… With the exception of those (generally very few) staff who have left under a cloud, most of your past staff members, especially those who have retired after long and loyal service, will almost certainly feel good about the organisation and want it to succeed into the future. Your alumni are, therefore, an important part of your PR machine. They are a free – and usually relatively untapped – source of experience and wisdom. Keep them informed and use them as a resource.

Talk about a good investment in talent retention, and real value for money… Like many others, we regularly appoint 'emeritus' positions who, we have found, for the cost of an office and a computer, give us enormous and ongoing commitment and tangible outputs – as well as sage advice and mentoring – perhaps for a decade or more. They love it and we love it. Work life doesn't stop at 65 or 70 for many 'cats'.

Looking back, revitalising our Alumni Association was one of my better moves. Not just for 'retirees' (many of whom continued to be wise ambassadors for our organisation) but also the 'still actives' who – in their new assignments on leaving – opened some important doors for us to new opportunities, and new talent.

Throughout higher education, for example, in recent years there has been increased commitment to building strong links with 'working' alumni once it was recognised that they can provide both mentoring support for existing students and financial support (through donations) for institutions. Further, in many cases, especially with graduates who had come into the institution from abroad, local alumni groups have proven to be valuable sources of career development opportunities.

Getting delegation right... One very effective way of making your time go further, motivating your team and getting results, is to commit to considered and measured delegation:

Give people responsibility and don't micromanage; trust them, and value their way of doing things – which inevitably will be different from yours. The outcomes are what count.

Delegating responsibility and then constantly interfering tends to bring out the worst in people.

Don't delegate and then send emails of advice.

However, notwithstanding the importance of boundary crossing (and collaboration), those to whom authority is delegated need clarity about where they can – and should – act, and where they shouldn't...

If you have a square surrounded by busy roads and a group of children playing there, they will migrate to the middle of the square. If you fence it off (i.e. set clear boundaries) they will use the whole area. Very few organisations do this well, but if you delegate clearly – and about twice as much as you think wise – accepting the occasional breaches and allowing great freedom of

> *decision making within the boundaries, you are most likely to enhance motivation and get strong performance.*

In other words, make sure your colleagues know exactly what they're on the line for, and that what they're doing is important, and that successful outcomes really matter to you. Relatedly, and as part of the framing of your delegating, it is also important to make it clear that there will be consequences if there is undue delay or inaction.

> *To bring out the best in people, it is important to have an agreed common purpose and then provide the maximum amount of autonomy and flexibility to allow staff to operate within those boundaries. If you try to exercise too much control, or don't have a common purpose or business reason behind your decisions, you will spend a lot of time debating decisions and demotivating people. You might spend time debating decisions anyway, but at least people will be more likely to have a common language and understand where your decisions are coming from.*

Further, there will be times when the need for formal delegation comes unexpectedly:

> *Good people will attract external commitments, often at short notice ("You need to join the Minister in Singapore on Tuesday.") This can often make the management of day-to-day life quite complex.*

All the more reason, therefore, to ensure that good delegation processes are in place, and that both your team and those who report directly to you are high quality and 'in the loop'. (See also Sections 8 and 9.)

Managing duality… In this complex, pressured, ambiguous and dilemma-filled world, we need to work with the 'and', not the 'or'. Thus, for example, it is usually best to nurture diverse perspectives, but these need to be channelled. We must be competitive but work in partnerships, action-oriented but reflective, planned but opportunistic. Change is critical, but so is the stability provided by continuity. Analysis is key, but so is making use of your intuition. Organisationally, we can appropriately centralise but empower through decentralisation; be big in scope and power but 'small' in terms of responsiveness.

The leader needs to be comfortable wearing 'bifocal glasses'... being comfortable looking into the future AND, at the same time, being able to ensure that today's results are delivered. Because without a successful today there may be no effective tomorrow for the organisation.

Those who lead need to harness schizophrenia... in the ballroom analogy – on the floor dancing but also up on the balcony observing.

You need to retain traditional academic values and modern management efficiencies, including increased external engagement.

Quality decision making... It is necessary to accept at a very early stage that, for all the areas where you are 'on the line', ultimately, you are principally responsible for the decisions that determine courses of action. There may be, and usually is, a collectivity of inputs. There may be delegation. But, at the end of the day, while the ownership can be shared, the 'buck' stops on the leader's desk. So...

Learn to focus on the 'so whats' (the outcomes if successful) of a project... not just the 'whats'. This is the essence of being a successful research leader/manager rather than just a paper-publishing researcher.

Usually it's worth thinking through, and perhaps discussing, the consequences – especially the possible unintended consequences – before agreeing to a proposal.

What brings out the worst in our people is arbitrary, non-evidenced-based and/or inconsistent decision making.

Even so...

What distinguishes a good leader from a great leader is their intuition.

Timing is all; and chance matters.

It is appropriate to trust gut feelings. Dr Ramesh Mashelkar, an elder statesman of Indian science, tells a very relevant story around a patent challenge in which he makes quite clear how an important decision was (actually) made:

> "How was this decision to challenge the patent taken? I remember reading the *Times of India* in my home in Delhi as I was having a cup of tea in the morning. I saw this news item. Some innovators from a university in the USA had been granted a patent on the wound-healing properties of turmeric. I was shocked. This was something that had been known in India for generations. Since it was prior knowledge, it did not fulfil the criteria of novelty, non-obviousness and utility, which are a must for the granting of a patent. I intuitively decided to fight it. I made a public announcement that same evening as a part of a public lecture at the National Physical Laboratory in Delhi. This was daring. I was Secretary to the Government of India, therefore I should have ideally secured several government permissions before announcing the challenge publicly. But I went entirely by my intuition and instincts and just announced the challenge. The rest is history – the patent was disallowed."

It is always worth remembering…

> "Chance favours the prepared mind."
> Louis Pasteur (1822-1895)

Additionally, honesty and transparency in decision making (and related communication) are also key. It tends to go down badly when there is (perceived) dishonesty or flummery around decisions, for example when questions are rightly asked around who actually took the decision, and why.

Clever people are much more willing to accept decisions they don't like if they are given a reasonable reason for the decision. Sometimes – even quite often – this will mean giving the objector some background information that he or she didn't have – often through circumstance, not through fault. So you need to have your antennae quite well-tuned to where the 'objecting audience' is coming from.

People want an answer – even if they don't like it. Avoiding taking the call, or ambiguity, is weak leadership. What people hate most is uncertainty.

Inactivity can frustrate. Don't take lack of complaint as support for inaction – often people merely sigh, and get on with their own thing. For this reason…

I've found that a willingness to make decisions is welcomed even if the decisions aren't to everyone's liking.

I remember, when I was a researcher, the research leaders who commanded greatest respect among my (then) colleagues were the ones who showed flexibility – a sense of not being hidebound by rules, but were willing to make bold decisions on the basis of common sense (and facts!), and to accept responsibility for the outcome. They were also decisive. We knew where we stood. They would listen carefully to a proposal and then make a decision (often involving disbursement from discretionary funds).

Issues must be grasped and not evaded:

Most headships of departments (in academic institutions) are rotational. So some Heads can be reluctant to take the really hard decisions: "Why do today what you can put off until tomorrow?" In consequence, the problems accumulate, or grow, over time because nobody is taking the tough calls.

Even people with long-term appointments can live by this maxim, by the way!

Academic leaders are sometimes reluctant to lead and to make a decision if they don't have complete consensus. Academics can be very skilled at 'constructive delays'.

Leaders tend to underestimate the time and money wasted when decisions are delayed or don't actually get made at all. It is seen all the time in the workplace – too many leaders in the public sector are paralysed with fear about making decisions. This is partly a legacy/culture issue, e.g. decision making by committee, and partly due to the ever-increasing personal risk for public sector leaders in the current political and economic environment.

Deciding whether or not to consult can also be problematic.

In general, be respectful, consult, listen and learn, get all to contribute ideas and guide opinion to a solution, but always with a relentless focus on quality. But, at the same time, you need to be very clear, and distinguish carefully between when you should (just) inform, versus consult, versus negotiate. They are quite different. And you should clearly signal which line you intend to follow, so that everybody knows.

Sometimes you need to take the approach: "The buck stops with me, and I've heard what you've all said, and now I'm making the decision." If this is said and done in a good way it can even be cheerfully accepted by the team.

Engagement and consultation are important – but there comes a time where you need to decide and get on with implementation. Realising that can be very liberating. In other words, your people need to see that – whatever you decide – you've listened seriously to all (relevant) points of view. You have to consult, but you have to decide.

And after the decision is taken it will usually be necessary to stand firm.

I was very influenced by a wonderful leader I once had who was a great change agent... and would make decisions, never if there was only narrow support but often if support was maybe a 70:30. Only once did all the '30 percents' coalesce into some quite fierce opposition. She was unmoved, stating that the only thing that the opposition had in common was dislike of her!

There will, however, be occasions when it quite quickly

becomes apparent that a decision that has been taken is wrong in part or in whole. Then it is best to acknowledge that and revisit the original decision. The worst course is to 'die in the ditch' and stubbornly persist with the erroneous position. Seeking to save face can be disastrous.

Handling failure… While it is comforting to expect every aspect of your role to run smoothly and successfully, this is usually – indeed very much – the exception rather than the rule…

> *In every high-tech organisation, you get mistakes and things fail. You need to be emotionally and intellectually prepared for this.*

But…

> *Blaming others for failures… is a certain path to perdition.*

> *Hanging someone out to dry when there has been a mess-up is a mistake. Clearly if and when there are persistent errors you need to deal with poor performance. But taking responsibility as the leader, and defending your team from unwarranted attack, will send an important message of your support to the rest of your troops.*

> *True leadership is most clearly revealed when others on your team make mistakes.*

> *As a leader you need to take responsibility for failure. And celebrate everyone else when there is success.*

> *When somebody fails, getting into the blame game is a disaster. Assuming it's not negligence, it's about saying – What have we learned from this? How can I help you, going forward?*

It is this latter sentiment that must be overriding.

> "He who has never failed somewhere, that man cannot be great." Herman Melville (1819-1891) American novelist, and author of *Moby-Dick*

Goal and role clarity… In addition – and closely related – to the ubiquitous 'communication problems' (see Section 9), conflict in the workplace can arise for a variety of reasons. Two, in particular.

Firstly, non-clarity around goals: "You think we should be headed there, but I think it should be over here…".

Having high and clearly-articulated – and agreed – objectives… brings out the best in people.

Secondly, non-clarity around roles: "You think this is my job; I think it's yours…"

"Winning this series would be great, but it is more important we get players' roles right and they feel comfortable." Justin Langer (1970-) Australian Cricket Coach, and former Test Match batsman.

Thus, clarifying just exactly where we're headed and 'Who's going to do what by when?' can save a lot of time and trouble.

Knowing yourself… So far we have concentrated primarily on the interactions between the leader/manager and his or her team, and the circumstances in which he or she is operating. While self-knowledge has been implicit, it is important to highlight some explicit observations:

When you know yourself well there are some things or behaviours you might need to suppress… If you are inclined to be pessimistic, suppress it – people need their leader to be optimistic about the future. (As a wise leader once said to me, "My job is to absorb uncertainty, and stop my people from being scared.") If you have a tendency to panic, suppress it – what you do and how you behave as a leader will be magnified, and they will think 'things must really be bad'. If you're somewhat introverted, suppress it – get out there and 'work the room', it's part of your leadership responsibilities.

But it is not all simply black and white. Taking note of the greyness can be valuable…

Many leaders suffer from impostor syndrome… "Can I really do this? It's surely just a matter of time before someone finds me out?" Knowing at an earlier time that it wasn't just me would have been reassuring.

The doubts you have are useful – to inform your current situation, and to be realistic about future possibilities.

Ask regularly: "Am I still committed to my goals?"

No one believes the leopard can change its spots… people still see me through the lens of my past behaviours.

And if you are looking to lead…

Leadership has to be intentional if it is to be effective – although one might inadvertently, or accidentally, or even belligerently, end up in a leadership role, to lead without intent is to be in a dangerous place.

You need to be very clear, in your own mind, why you want the leadership position. And what it is you're looking for. I wanted to make change happen.

What motivated me to get into a leadership role in the first place? To do it better than I'd seen it done.

Time in a leadership position only reinforces what one knew at the start – but it's so important – integrity is everything. You lead by permission, not by rank or authority. You lose that permission if your motives are doubted.

Leadership translates into high visibility in all things that you do. If you do not want visibility, do not lead. Knowing this is an important part of the decision-making process that we often do not have the opportunity to consider before becoming a leader.

And do remember that there is a great deal of difference between leading a team that you've grown yourself and leading a team that's been foisted upon you as you've moved 'up'. You need to work hard at finding ways in which you can inspire, and provide a sense of purpose, that also works for you. Authenticity is key. When you take over a new team it is not a popularity contest. You need to be very clear on intent but very open to feedback.

On leadership 'versus' management... In essence, good leadership has two major and inter-related characteristics. You need to have a vision, clearly articulated, and you need to bring people along. But you also need to be able to operationalise this, which will include getting engaged in the necessary detail. The leadership 'versus' management debate is a false dichotomy – you have to be able to do both.

> "The engine room and the strategy are really the yin and the yang. You can't have one without the other and we run them in parallel... " Catherine Livingstone (1955-) Chair, Commonwealth Bank of Australia and Chancellor of the University of Technology Sydney; and formerly Chair of CSIRO and Telstra, and President of the Business Council of Australia.

The value of networking... The more senior you get, the lonelier it often becomes:

> *It would have been good to have been warned about the loneliness of leadership before I experienced it.*

Having an external network, which works in mentoring mode and involves people who have 'been there, done that', can be highly valuable. Participation with colleagues and peers from different institutions, or different parts of your own organisation – for example, in leadership development training – can build a long-lasting support and advice network. Working with kindred spirits with empathetic shoulders to cry on when it's crying time can be beneficial.

> *I learnt very quickly that I hardly had anyone to talk to – so I used a new vice-chancellor from a nearby university.*

Networking better enables us to benchmark. For example:

- are we suffering from hubris?
- are we as good as we think – and say – we are?

- are we as well-connected as we should be?

Since taking up the top job, I've visited a dozen of my opposite numbers running universities – it's one of the best time-investments I've made. For example, cross-calibrating on what's 'hot' in education or research, and comparing notes on the trials and tribulations of herding cats. And looking for opportunities to work together – most big grants are multi-university these days. I'm pushing all my executive and deans to do the same. I'm preaching 'network, network, network'.

'Outside' visits – even (sometimes especially) in one's own institution – are invaluable. Three things may emerge:

- hitherto unidentified opportunities for collaboration;
- objective feedback or advice on problems, which can help hugely (and comes for free)
- 'creative plagiarism': "That's a very good idea, I'll try it in my place."

Push hard, therefore, but with the full understanding that…

As you encourage your good people to network and work collaboratively, their own talent will get spotted and temptations (to leave) will surely come their way. C'est la vie. You then just have to work harder to help them excel and be happy with you.

Building trust… Trust is important. You build trust in small, bite-sized chunks, but you can destroy it in one fell swoop. As we say elsewhere: "Trust is the air that good relationships breathe".

I am very cautious in my people- and culture-related decisions. It takes a day to mess up morale, and a year to fix it. Inclusivity and transparency are key – harder work but a better chance of success.

You demonstrate trust by delegating responsibility appropriately (and here, think 'more not less') and through showing loyalty to stand by your staff members when they don't deliver the outcome you'd hoped for, despite their best efforts.

If the project succeeds, the project leader is on the podium. If it fails I'm on the podium. People have got to know: "We are behind you. We believe in you."

On power... There is often a temptation to believe that, as a leader, you are in charge and your position is one of power and influence. This is, of course, true to some extent, but...

The idea that you are there in absolute control is totally misleading.

Leading in a university is an odd job. Most of the pleasures – and they are real – are vicarious, experienced through the successes of others; most of the achievements are by stealth.

"The presidential power that seems so vast and indeed so excessive to many outside the White House appears all too small and shrunken to Presidents and their aides when compared to the stupendous burdens put on the White House." James MacGregor Burns (1918-2014) Presidential biographer and Pulitzer Prize winner.

And a final thought... Whatever you do, don't pretend to know when you don't – you will always be found out. And your credibility will be lost.

Saying "I don't know" or "Please explain this to me", in other words admitting your ignorance, can be a good thing – far from being seen as failure, people like explaining things to the boss.

5. COMPOSURE under pressure and the implementation imperative

"Genius is one percent inspiration, and ninety-nine percent perspiration." Thomas Edison (1847-1931)

Sticking to the game plan (and staying calm)... Tenacity and staying power are all-important. Leaders and managers need to have a very strong sense of purpose, combined with an ability to recognise problems as they arise. And when it comes to problems, it is usually helpful to obey the sign spotted in a local lift: "If there is a problem, stay calm". And remember the old Rudyard Kipling poem 'If' which starts "If you can keep your head when all about you are losing theirs, and blaming it on you" – because, as one of our colleagues remarked, "Calmness is a vital, core response skill in a leader".

To succeed in management around here you need an ordered mind. You can't be a stressful person. You need to be a pretty calm type, to cope with the volume and the short deadlines.

Also, from the point of view of the team, it is necessary for them to see that you are not easily deflected from the agreed path.

Because the lead times for successful change to embed are so long, the hardest – and most important – thing, I've found, is sticking to the unrelenting, unwavering belief in our strategy, and riding over the bumps of inevitable perturbation, when sometimes, in the short term, it may look as if you've got it wrong.

"Leadership is all about composure under pressure and sticking to the game plan." John Eales (1970-) former Australia rugby captain.

Obviously we're not talking dogmatic 'Charge of the Light Brigade' commitment.

The change process is like dancing – if you never take any steps backwards it's boring.

Thus you are likely to need to exercise some well-judged flexibility from time to time – one door might shut and another open; there are usually a number of different ways to achieve your overarching goals.

Plan well… "Be Prepared" – the Boy Scouts' motto. On the other hand…

"We don't have a plan, so nothing can go wrong."
Spike Milligan (1918–2002) British comedian.

You need, first, to arm yourself with the sense of purpose. It is then necessary to ensure that there is focused commitment to delivery. This needs a delivery plan. An understanding of the rudiments of project management is likely to be helpful but this certainly doesn't mean handing over the planning responsibility to an 'expert'. However, the exception here would be in mission-critical developments – for example, the literature abounds with reports of major IT projects which have lost their way, gone frighteningly over budget, and in the end failed to deliver the planned outcomes because of inexpert management.

In putting in a major, new, enterprise-wide information system, I was advised to think 'times pi' – that is: "If you're not careful, it will take you about three times as long as you thought it would, and probably cost three times as much as you budgeted." Anticipating this, we put much better controls around delivery and deadlines, and around budgeting and expenditure.

Finding the balance between thoughtfully structured planning within the team and professionally facilitated project management is an art that needs to be developed.

The techniques for managing projects well, whether they are large and transformational or small and incremental, have not varied since Rome was built, but are continuously forgotten. In addition to well-structured pre-planning, the most common element forgotten is clear accountability – in other words, clearly assigned follow-up actions and responsibilities.

We should have been more reflective and better planned around the management of our change processes – a key task of leadership.

But try not to overdo it; sometimes very simple approaches will suffice…

The more formal and comprehensive project management methodologies are not usually applicable to our (smaller scale) research environments – we're not building jumbo jets or nuclear accelerators. It's not a widely-accepted view, but the backs of envelopes, or napkins in the tea-room, have worked really well in my career. The exception, by observation, being major IT or building projects – then you bring in the serious, professional project managers or you end up in big trouble.

Implementation excellence… Effective execution is an imperative. Ninety-five per cent of all the decisions we take stand or fall on the success – or otherwise – of the quality and timeliness of the implementation process.

"Vision without execution is hallucination."
Thomas Edison (1847-1931)

Having a well-articulated view of your operating environment – your 'current reality' as they say – you need to separate out strategic intent (what to do) from strategic execution (how to do it). The latter is almost always more difficult, and where most of us fail.

Execution excellence must be an all-out attack… All you need is clarity, ownership, focus and connectedness around just a few key goals, with effective cascading and line of sight 'down' to the bench, with success measures in place and 'cradle to grave' performance management; in other words goals plus measures plus performance review integrated across organisation-unit-individual levels. But, wow, if only it were this easy…!

No matter how elegant the strategic or policy solution (to a problem or opportunity) is, it is worthless unless it can be delivered effectively – separating strategy or policy development from implementation often leads to a poor outcome… You need to have structures and processes in place to systematically connect creative policy development and its execution.

"A vision is worth little if the President doesn't have the character – the courage and heart – to see it through." Peggy Noonan (1950-) speech writer to former President Ronald Reagan.

Small steps?… How to get there – the detail of implementation – is often not clear at the start. But the leisure of waiting for the great launch is not normally available – it is essential for things to start to happen:

When you don't know how to take the big steps, first take the most sensible little step.

Keep the problem grand while making the steps to the solution small… having researchers plodding towards a far-off goal will initially be motivating by its scope, but people become disenchanted by its distance unless small goals are met – and celebrated – along the way.

In the change process, if you have no signs of success in three years then you have failed. You need small success stories all the way along.

Organising arrangements… The conventional wisdom is that 'structure follows strategy', that is, your organising arrangements should support effective strategy implementation. While modifying your structure may well help you deliver on your strategic goals – potentially more rapidly and effectively than through the prevailing organising arrangements – be careful to look before you leap into extensive restructuring.

By the time they reach senior positions, many leaders will have seen the quotation, often attributed (some would say erroneously) to the Roman writer, Petronius Arbiter (27-66 CE) Roman courtier and satirist:

> "We trained hard…but it seemed that every time we were beginning to form up into teams, we would be reorganised. I was to learn later in life that we tend to meet any new situation by reorganising; and a wonderful method it can be for creating the illusion of progress while producing confusion, inefficiency, and demoralisation."

Whether the attribution is correct or not is by the by; the sentiment provides an important cautionary message.

The more complicated an organisation is, the better communication must be.

Where the devil resides… While it is tempting as 'the leader' to concentrate only around the 'big picture', this can be risky. An awareness of the ways in which implementation can go wrong is needed; in most cases this originates among the 'small' things:

Effective leadership and management of an institution requires a capacity for attention to detail, and for completing processes so that they will work, for ensuring that functions work, even in the smallest units where services are delivered.

> "Never neglect details." General Colin Powell (1937-) former US Secretary of State.

And what gets measured… gets done, so says the old, and useful, adage. But be careful about getting carried away with this.

> "Not everything that can be counted counts, and not everything that counts can be counted." Albert Einstein (1879-1955)

It is foolish indeed to insist on objectives and targets and measures that then totally prescribe people's behaviour. This is not the way to run research, although it might be the way to run a supermarket – though even then I doubt it.

And 'less is more' – absolutely – when it come to metrics. But it is also essential to ensure that those you use are meaningful, clearly articulated and well-communicated...

I was surprised when that country's Minister of Science and Technology indicated to me, over a glass of wine, that his prime measures of performance for the major research organisation for which he had oversight responsibility were: they stay on budget; they don't embarrass me in the media; and they provide me with some good news stories from time to time that my Cabinet colleagues might enjoy.

Certainly these are rather loose metrics in conventional terms, but they illustrate the point that there is a need to try to find measurable outcomes. Increasingly, there is a tendency to see the use of 'metrics' as a catch-all solution to measuring implementation effectiveness – even to the point of their becoming an end in themselves. As well as that, irrelevant or inappropriate metrics can be more dangerous than no metrics at all, since they can distort the outcomes:

Metrics are really difficult. Often huge reliance is placed on them; but academics don't want to be measured by input and output – they believe they're doing something more special than that. Metrics have their place, but they should never be the sole criteria for judgement.

Metrics need to be relevant and aligned with the values and behaviours you expect from an organisation.

Metrics are important. And while the prevailing dominant indicators of university performance are the international rankings, initially dominated by research outputs in international journals, over time these rankings have broadened the range of measures used. For example, one much used ranking – the QS University World Ranking – currently takes account of not only academic and research reputation but also employer reputation, staff/student ratio, numbers of citations, numbers of international staff and numbers of international students. However, on the other hand, and as previously mentioned, 'impact' *per se* remains seriously neglected, although some windows have recently been opening a little, especially in regard to increasingly acknowledging 'tech transfer' as a viable and important component of an academic's portfolio of activities, and corresponding performance assessment.

Let's not forget the old saying: "You tell me how you're going to measure me, and I'll tell you how I'm going to behave."

Following through on performance is critical... At the nominal conclusion of the implementation process, or at a key milestone, it is not sufficient to smile comfortably and simply close the book. There needs to be active follow-up. And, in line with the maxim, "Feedback is the food of champions":

> *When I failed, it was when I didn't hold people to account. Maybe giving feedback was too hard, or I didn't make it important enough to invest the time, or they were valuable and I thought I might offend and then lose them. Whatever... It was always a mistake.*

> *I've seen some frustrated colleagues, late 40s or early 50s, who haven't made it to the top, and won't, even though they'd like to, and probably have the inherent competence to do so. But they were let down by some boss or other, ten or even twenty years before, who failed to be frank and honest with them around some of their key flaws. Fixable back then, but entrenched now. And I've seen other highflyers get frank, no-holds-barred feedback, early in their careers and it strengthens their wings. It worked for me.*

> *Striving to be the best we can be requires us to continually seek constructive critiquing and feedback on how we can improve.*

> *When someone has already made up their mind that they've got the right answer, it's too late for criticism. It will often then be seen as destructive. You need a process to expose people to critique when their ideas are still developing – and you can add value, or even re-direct.*

Then the feedback/criticism is usually seen as constructive. It's a great way to see ideas expand, and people grow. It's a bit like working with building blocks, as opposed to chipping away at something that's already been built.

Although this is far from easy, it is important because…

Researchers and academics tend to be optimistic, therefore they can mislead each other, and themselves. They can have rose-coloured glasses around how good they are.

Have patience: it all takes time… Particularly when you take on organisational change, 'it' always takes much, much longer than you think it will. Remember – as one observer put it – the internet took twenty years to become an overnight success!

I've come to realise that what we set out to do here cannot be achieved in the tenure of a single Vice-Chancellor.

Your achievements probably will not really be known for five to ten years – and they will depend upon how successful your successor is.

6. COMMITTEES etc.

Committees are, or can appear to be, the life-blood of academic and research communities. But they can also proliferate like weeds, and resolutely resist abolition.

I'm an abolisher of committees. Like one of my folk heroes – a politician, as it happens – did when he came into power, I abolished all the committees and made them talk themselves back into existence. Very few of them managed to.

There is, of course, a place for committees but they must have real work to do, a tight brief, and clear reporting deadlines. You will need to do your homework around the selection of the membership and, particularly, the selection of the Chair. In the academic world, major committees, such as university senates, can in fact be…

…great places for preventing fires starting, by opening up contentious issues. The occasional and well-judged vote can also give you a real sense of the mood, and how strong it is.

Some committees are needed in order to provide decision-making mechanisms – but those involved must be well informed – perceptions and attitudes are important – so somewhere along the line it is essential to get the right people involved and consulted – committees can do this.

But all too often committees don't deliver on expectations:

"The appointment of a [committee] 'to consider what means, if any, can be discovered to prevent the Public Washing of Linen'…[results in] the formation of an invertebrate body which sits for two years, with growing discomfort, on the clothes-basket containing the linen. When the [committee] is so stupefied that it has quite forgotten what it is sitting on, it issues three minority reports, of enormous bulk, on some different subject. The reports are referred to the Council… and [thereafter] to the wastepaper basket. This is called 'reforming the University from within'." Francis Cornford (1874-1943)

Committees are an aid to management, not a substitute for it.

You can't manage through committees... you can only manage through people.

We established a committee to manage cross-institution infrastructure. It didn't work. You need a person in charge.

And as for managing committee meetings themselves, it is quite surprising how badly this is often done:

"Meetings... made the Mad Hatter's Tea Party seem like a paradigm of positive decision-making." David Lodge (*Changing Places*, 1975)

Are committees a necessary evil?... Regrettably this would seem to be the case. But, in thinking about committees, and as observed above, you should decide whether they are needed at all. Often a job that needs to be done is time-limited, then the work can be done effectively by an ad hoc working party or task group that is itself time-limited. This can be a step towards simplification and, in this context, there is advantage in keeping the committee arrangements under review.

In restructuring our governance arrangements we went from 50+ committees, with some 'spaghetti' inter-relationships, to just ten. Everyone was delighted.

Despite the downsides, however, one of the beneficial roles a committee can play is that of oversight, fostering a sense of participation, democracy, openness and transparency in decision making. Ideally, the committee is broadly representative, but may meet only infrequently in which case power to act is often delegated to the Chair or a small working group drawn from the committee. Then the work and decision making is carried out in ways that are subject to the tacit consent of the whole committee. All such decisions are rapidly (note: rapidly) communicated to the members by circular. Any member who wishes may object, and request a meeting to consider any of the 'decisions'. If the chair is performing competently and has the respect and confidence of the committee, such objections may be rare, but the real possibility of challenging any decision that is dubious or seems to require further consideration gives a sense of collegiality and joint decision making.

Meetings Management 101... The most basic advice on running committees makes it evident that this is an art form, especially in its chairing. Committee meetings are different from 'meetings', *per se,* which are, of course, part and parcel of getting the job done, whether they are regular staff meetings and the like, or opportunity- or challenge-focused brain-storming sessions.

And certain 'principles' apply all round:

> *First and foremost, around meetings, my mantra is 'Do we need a meeting?'*

If the answer is 'Yes', then you need to clarify the nature of the meeting, and possibly of each particular agenda item. Specifically:

> *The purpose of meetings (and agenda items therein) often get confused. For example: Is this a decision-making meeting? Or merely consultation? Or is the meeting (or the agenda item) just information sharing? Then again, maybe it's just brainstorming.*

> *Often, it's very useful to clarify up front: 'What are we talking about here?'*

Next, if you do need a meeting, who do you need at the meeting? And why?

> *Too often people who don't need to be there are at meetings, wasting your time and theirs. Conversely, when the key decision maker(s) can't make it, everyone else is just marking time.*

Discipline is, therefore, basic in creating a productive meetings culture. Be clear 'from the top' that if Fred can't make a particular session, for whatever reason, he has to live with the decisions and actions resulting from the meeting. And you will need to work hard not to be continuously changing meeting times to accommodate player X, Y or Z:

> *Changing meeting times is a cottage industry around here. It keeps the PAs gainfully employed for maybe half their time!*

> *Most research organisations are not good at operations – that is describing what you're going to do and then living up to it. We're now much more rigorous about reviewing milestones, and we start and end our meetings on time. People are not generally used to this discipline but they learn quickly.*

Committees need to meet, so invest quality time in crafting the agenda. Start, and end, the meeting on time. Nurture inclusivity – encouraging all participants to contribute. To this end, whether Chair or member, read the papers beforehand and get organised.

As with most endeavours, preparation is key. For example, does everyone concerned know what the meeting is about? Has the agenda been circulated in advance? Have any necessary papers also been circulated in advance, giving people enough time to read them. Be righteously indignant if there is an inadequate notice period for advanced digestion. And expect others to be righteously indignant if *you* slip up in this regard. Progress can be made if careful thought is given to the preparation of the papers for the meeting, especially for those 'big ones'.

> *We started making some good progress when we restructured and colour-coded the Council papers. We used a cover page (white) – which explained the purpose of the paper and indicated recommendations, with implications. Backup pages (blue) are desirable reading with basic information on background, issue(s) defined, process, conclusions, recommend-ations, implications – including resourcing require-ments, follow-up actions,*

together with account-abilities and timescales. Supporting pages (pink) provide all the detailed information and data that could be drawn upon to support the Backup pages. We found very quickly that the members of our Council could then better prioritise their approach to meetings.

One of the important advance tasks for the Chair is to decide who comes to the meeting, fully recognising that they come with different perspectives, have different styles, can contribute in different ways. And these different qualities need to be harnessed.

The Chair plays a key role in stopping people dominating the conversation and in pulling in the often more quiet people to make a contribution…

One of the problems with meetings is that people often don't listen. They just wait for an opportunity to make their point. One fun thing to do, now and again, is making a rule that you can only talk when you have summarised adequately the point made by the previous person (and to his or her satisfaction). Sometimes this takes more than one attempt! This slows things down of course but has useful consequences.

The Chair should aim to summarise proceedings after each agenda item, specifying the decision taken and follow-up action required, with clearly-defined responsibilities, and timescales. This should go without saying (but rarely does). Minutes of the meeting should be out in draft as soon as possible (this really matters, and 72 hours is a good guideline) and be given to the Chair to review and turn around in a day. After ratification, they should go immediately to the other committee members. Minutes that arrive two days before the next meeting (quite likely a month or so later) are no use: no one will remember whether they are accurate or not, and they cannot act as an action-memo for recalcitrant members who did not make a note of the jobs they were supposed to do.

As we say, all this should go without saying, but rarely does.

Key success factors for review committees... Quite a different domain is occupied by those committees or taskforces set up to carry out a very specific role – such as a review of the effectiveness of a particular department or activity. In addition to the careful selection of the participating members, the Key Success Factors – which might, incidentally, also apply to more general committee work – should include:

- a tight brief, agreed beforehand by the reviewers and the reviewees.
- careful selection of the Chair.
- well-thought-through briefing material. Be prepared to stamp down on the 'overkill' submission from those to be reviewed in which absolutely everything is dropped on the unsuspecting reviewers... Remember the ironic observation (often attributed to Mark Twain but most likely originated by Blaise Pascal in 1657) : "I haven't got time to write you a short letter so I've written you a long one".
- rapid turn-around time on the draft report, for member scrutiny and, thereafter, timely finalisation.
- subsequent, senior-level monitoring, for example, after six or twelve months, to ensure that the approved recommendations have been, or are being, effectively implemented. And – most importantly – not forgetting to feed this progress back to the review members. Nothing is more galling for a review group than feeling that their hard work and precious time has gone into the proverbial black hole.

Review fatigue... If you are not careful, reviewing can be become a business in its own right and something of a substitute for management.

We were, probably indisputably, the best department in the country. But across seven years we had to run six major reviews: two cycles of a research assessment exercise; two cycles of professional accreditation; one government-led teaching quality assessment; and one university internal assessment. This was just not a good use of our time.

But, with the increasing emphasis on accountability, reviewing is likely to be part of the scene for the foreseeable future.

Keep the Chair informed… Focused reviews can have unpredictable outcomes. At times observations and recommendations are not at all what was expected, and seriously bad news can sometimes be uncovered. Whatever the story, never – ever – hide (or 'spin') bad news from members of your governing body, and especially not from its Chair. If there is trouble around the corner he or she should be given the courtesy of 'no surprises'. Bad news will always come out, often with an emphasis that makes it seem worse that it really is. Most individuals who rise to this level of governance are pretty aware, and know only too well, that in all organisations, things go wrong. Sometimes very wrong. Trust is the air that good relationships breathe, remember. Not 'telling it how it is' is a sure-fire way to undermine this.

You also need to be very clear about getting bad news early – and that hiding things is not acceptable. (They often get worse, anyway!) It's about saying "OK, so now we're going to develop a solution together."

On governance and ethics… This is currently a hot topic, especially following the global financial crisis and the 'failure of governance' that seems to make media headlines all too regularly. But governance issues have in recent years involved much more than economic and financial governance. Debates about identity politics, prejudice, and perceived and unconscious bias have permeated institutions.

'Governance' (if you are a cat) might feel like 'what those people up there do' which is mostly…

Listening – to management, staff, external stakeholders, etc. – and reacting, offering counsel, challenging and giving or withholding support for major decisions. Maybe one per cent of what a Board (or Executive Committee) actually does is being proactive, most notably in the appointment (or renewal, or termination) of the Chief Executive Officer.

Typically, as the organisation's 'highest authority', it is the Board, the Executive Committee or their equivalent, that oversees and orchestrates governance. Here the principles articulated previously, especially those emphasising the need to get the best Chair, are germane.

One time, we (in management) just knew that the Chairman being mooted was the wrong call. This is dangerous territory but we persisted and got our point across. The alternative appointee did a brilliant job.

In an organisation, the typical committee structures – for example, the Audit Committee, the Remuneration Committee, the Risk Committee, etc. – provide the mechanics of governance. In actual practice, good (or bad) governance pervades each and every level of business and is, like most of what we have been dealing with so far, very much dependent on specific people and their relationships with each other.

An issue which merits special mention in this regard is the nature of the relationship between the Chair and senior Executive Officers in systems where these roles are separated.

The Chair has to be both a mentor and a shoulder to cry on. But the Chair must also be strong enough to control the behaviour of protégés. Relationships between the executive team and the Board are always interesting.

Good communication and trust-building 'upwards management' are, therefore, core skills of the cat herder and Chief Executive Officer. 'No surprises' is a good Golden Rule.

Another imperative is to keep a sense of perspective around values and ethics "when all about you are losing theirs", sometimes no easy task in our highly competitive world, with ongoing pressure for 'results' – and, particularly, for bottom-line performance.

Confronted with almost daily examples of how badly people can behave in professional situations, you must be a role model for ethical behaviour. A strong vision is needed at high level to marry the demands for short-term results with the long-term 'public good'.

> *Quality ethics is about marrying the short term with the long term. Whether it be pressure (temptation?) to manipulate accounts, or to turn a bit of a blind eye to pollution, instilling ethical behaviour demands longer-term thinking.*

> *We need to ensure that short-term expediency is tempered by a clear view of long-term impacts. In the modern world, unethical behaviour will in due course be 'outed' and have repercussions.*

> *There was a celebrated judgement, a while back, around a failed major, national, financial institution where the presiding judge remarked: "I found myself rhetorically asking: did anyone stand back and ask themselves the simple question 'is this right?'"*

A very good question indeed.

7. Managing the CASH

The ability to marshal financial resources is critical to success.

If you are given leadership responsibility without authority, especially over the relevant finances, it is highly likely that you will be left to languish.

When push comes to shove, there is good reason to conclude that leading and managing comes down to seeking institutional security and, primarily, financial security. For those in senior leadership, getting the finances right is a crucial matter.

And, as Mr Micawber so persuasively remarked in Charles Dickens's *David Copperfield*: "Annual income twenty pounds, annual expenditure nineteen pounds nineteen and six, result happiness. Annual income twenty pounds, annual expenditure twenty pounds ought and six, result misery."

It's (always) a tough climate... There is an inclination amongst academics and researchers to assume, when faced with demanding financial circumstances, that this is a ground-breaking experience. Closer examination of the typical financial climate over past decades shows quite clearly that pressure on resources is the norm. The demands of research and academic development inevitably exceed the resources available, and this therefore requires careful appraisal and management of those resources.

There is never enough money – but there used to be.

"Do more with less." We hear this all the time.

So while (often expensive) equipment and talented people are undoubtedly central to research progress, Lord Kelvin's wisdom remains germane: "We don't have all the resources, therefore we have to think."

Cutting back... Managing resources means not only the evaluation of the relative merits of different research programmes and educational initiatives, but also that choices need to be made. As we emphasise later on, meaningful strategy normally demands a reallocation of resources.

> *When it comes to making difficult choices… it is made more difficult when, from time to time, successful projects and/or people have to be cut back to allow the resources for the extraordinary opportunity.*

Some programmes will therefore need to contract, others to expand; new programmes will need to be created. This should be a process informed by the strategic direction of the organisation. Making the choices is not the most difficult part; the difficult issues are those associated with implementing such choices.

> *When it comes to budget cuts, starting new programmes is easy; terminating old programmes is hard.*

How often have we seen someone riding their proverbial hobby horse – making the case for continuing their current actions in pursuit of their "Tomorrow, just you wait and see" 10-years-on programme? But this horse has got two broken legs, it has gone blind, and all its hair is falling out. It needs a ceremonial (and urgent) shooting. Not easy, unless you can persuade the riders that: "Here is this wonderful new horse and we need your riding skills…" Switching from a favoured domain to take up new challenges is seen by many to be fraught with difficulty.

> *It's always much easier – and ultimately very much more successful – to pull people than push them, especially where you've had past wins, but you're into diminishing returns. Set up an attractive place where they can see themselves, declare success (and don't say 'it's not sensible that we're still doing this'!). Then move on.*

Your (personal) skill set… If it is accepted that all academic and research environments have, at their core, vital issues of resourcing, then it should be also accepted that the effective leader and manager will need to be financially literate. Thus, when you come into a senior post, it is essential to acquire the necessary skills as a matter of some urgency. This does not mean that you need to qualify hurriedly as a management accountant on the side, but you must be able easily to read and understand sets of accounts, balance sheets, and so on, and to comment sensibly – particularly in debates with colleagues who may feel that they know it all.

It's amazing how many people think they understand finance, and our finances. And they find it very easy to spend other people's money.

As I moved through the ranks, my weakness around 'matters financial' was becoming problematic. So I elected to join a senior leadership development program but with a financial slant – joining bankers, investment advisers, economic consultants and the like. The first two weeks nearly killed me! But by the end of the program I knew enough never again to be blindsided, or have the proverbial wool pulled over my eyes, in this whole area.

There are other skills that need to be understood. For example,

Competent leaders do need to get comfortable around digital technologies... issues brought to the fore during the 2020 pandemic of digital teaching, research and administration. There's all the digital infrastructure – massive computers, data analytics, simulation and modelling tools, etc. – that's needed in a modern research environment. Quality expertise on your team is increasingly important.

But always remember that, while there are some dangers in this area of being too dependent on the experts, this concern should not be a substitute for ensuring that you have highly skilled professional support.

Getting good help... In the whole finance domain there is one crucial piece of advice – and we give it based on some bad (and some good) experiences: Get at the top the VERY best financial person that you can possibly find and afford. A (much) broader thinker than the average number cruncher; someone interested in the wider organisation and in people; and someone with good communication skills. It is significantly beneficial to both you and your colleagues to have, as part of the team, an expert who is committed to the demystification of financial matters.

> *Get to know and learn how to get help from smart finance people. Specifically... never ask for money... always ask for advice. If they give you advice... then they have bought into your project... and, sometimes, financial support follows... after all, it is now their project, too!*

There have also been changes in other areas where getting in top quality talent can be really advantageous. We have just mentioned IT support; 'development' (generally meaning 'fund raising') is another example. Thus 'Development Officers', primarily focused on securing philanthropic support through building enduring relationships with external individuals and groups so as to gain increased financial support for agreed academic priorities, demand a special set of skills and experience.

Manna from (commercial) heaven?... Building on earlier comments we have made in the 'commercialisation' arena (Section 3), governments in particular have, almost universally, adopted the stance of expecting academic and research organisations to contribute to solving problems arising from financial constraints by raising income from the exploitation of intellectual property (IP). This is, to some degree, a right and proper expectation, but the income you can make from licensing or selling IP is, more often than not, significantly overestimated.

> *When thinking about selling IP I am always reminded of the observation of a science Nobel Laureate that among the principal ways of losing money – wine is the most pleasurable, but technology is the most certain!*
>
> *Everyone will tell you their one great success story of revenue-generating IP. In actuality it is very rare, particularly considering the amount of time and money invested in technology development.*

This is not to underplay the importance of public-funded institutions finding and nurturing partnerships to help ensure the effective application of new discoveries; but to do so without recognising the possible pitfalls is not wise.

Patents are worth the amount of money you are prepared to spend defending them.

'Vanity patents', e.g. for CV purposes, abound.

You can invest up to the proof-of-concept stage. Thereafter, you need the money men. And be assured that they will probably exploit you.

As a general rule, keep the inventors away from running a commercialised business. It's usually not their skill set.

Making the call… Later we build on the premise that 'strategy is about choice' and emphasise that implementing your chosen strategy won't happen unless some shift in resources takes place, to underpin your chosen priorities.

'Resources', of course, are not just about money; they are also about your people and how they spend their time. As far as the money is concerned, choosing from a number of possible alternatives, both on the expenditure and revenue sides, will be key. Two guiding observations may assist…

Don't spread the pain. When cuts are necessary it is important to recognise that 'equal misery' is not really a strategy. 'Selective misery' is difficult and requires careful planning but it is very much to the longer term benefit of the institution. It can provide an opportunity to put in place measures that should probably have happened before. And to invest properly in where your strategy tells you the future lies.

Investment advisers typically advocate a portfolio approach to managing risk. Being careful about putting all (or most of) your eggs in one basket is wise. For example, I observed some sister institutions relying hugely on international students' fees (for cross funding key research programmes) but when the political environment changed significantly numbers dwindled leaving a huge hole in their budgets.

The importance of elbow room... Access to discretionary funding is important since it provides the leader with the ability to respond quickly to proposals that, in his or her judgement, warrant immediate support. The size of the discretionary, developmental fund is not as important as its existence, although it must be sufficient to enable real things to be achieved. It should be used in a disciplined way and, in the best-regulated organisations, in a way that is consistent with overall financial security.

> *Since money is probably your most important, and perhaps only, tool (e.g. for introducing change)... you need financial discipline to create the necessary flexibility.*

> *If you don't get the money right you can't do anything; if you do, then you can always do something.*

GETTING THE JOB DONE – In Conclusion

As a leader, your job is to get results. First off, therefore, you had best make sure that there is crystal clarity as to what constitutes success – to and from those 'above' you, as well as down to those 'below'. If you don't achieve this, severe differences of opinion are inevitable down the track. In addition, the clarity you achieve will help you define your goals. Opaqueness and complexity can give rise to real problems here. On this journey, small wins – and celebrating them – are helpful.

Preparation is important, but so is fast on-the-job learning. Get away from your office, whenever possible. Listen hard – across and up and down your organisation and, most particularly, to your key external stakeholders. Make sure you know those that might harm you, and those that can help you. And work hard to build relationships, and trust.

Consult, therefore, but accept that there must be limits. Be decisive. As far as possible be evidence-based, but also trust your intuition. Plan well, but be tactically flexible around ways of reaching your strategic goals.

Delegate, where you have trust, and more than you might think is necessary. But take care to attend to ensuring both role-clarity and goal-clarity (who's going to do what, and by when). But don't abdicate or even step back from your responsibilities: follow up, and follow through, including being meticulous over the necessary details. 'Execution excellence' is a hallmark of successful leaders.

Think twice (three times, four times?) before pulling the lever of organisational structural change.

Like salt, use committees sparingly, when you have to. Tight script, tight paperwork (in and out), with support from the best Chair you can find.

Finally, you may have a great strategy, be wonderfully skilled with your people, but resources, or rather lack of them, can bring you down. Money still makes the world go round. And you will never have enough. Also, at the end of the day, it is probably your only real tool for getting the changes you want implemented. If you don't speak the 'language', learn to converse, fast. And make sure you have those with top finance skills at your shoulder.

C: MANAGING THE PEOPLE

While many in both academic and research life object to being considered part of a 'business', many of the larger institutions of higher education and research approach – or exceed – billion-dollar enterprises. As such, the perennial, and in our view appropriate, maxim "all business is people business" applies.

Thus, by design, this part of the book is central to our purpose. In it we seek to address the key issues germane to the recruitment, retention, deployment and motivation of your people.

We are convinced of the importance of talent in achieving success. *Inter alia*, therefore, we address the following: the key traits of your talent pool – excellence, enthusiasm, judgement; the trials and tribulations of picking people (and of sometimes having to let them go); and developing your people, managing performance and building your team.

We also deal with the priority aspect of communication – the root of many problems when it is done badly. Nevertheless, as one of our colleagues rightly labels it, communication is *the* 'cornerstone' of leadership.

Finally, we emphasise the grossly underutilised weapon in your 'talent war' armoury – that of recognition, of giving credit where it is due, both formally and informally. And the consequences of doing it poorly or unfairly.

All business is people business. Read on.

8. COLLEAGUES, not subordinates ("It's all about the people")

In the long run it's all about the talent.

The effective management of your people – recruitment, development, deployment, motivation, retention, your 'talent pipeline' – is your single most important sustainable advantage. Next to getting the strategy right, it must, therefore, be your number one management priority.

This is military campaign stuff – we truly are in a talent 'war'.

Thus, keep your eye (and focus) on this very important ball...

We were spending so much time on the detail around budgets, trying to get them to balance. Meanwhile good people were leaving.

The challenge of keeping our best talent is all-encompassing for us. There are so many great opportunities around the world.

Unleashing potential... It is not enough just to have talent in your organisation, you need to nurture the conditions in which that talent can thrive.

"You can't motivate people. That door is locked from the inside. You can, however, create a climate in which most of your people will motivate themselves to help the organisation to reach its objectives." Robert Townsend (1920-1998) President and CEO of Avis.

Provide care, and context. Unleash, stop constraining. You'll get linear improvement in performance.

In contrast...

What brings out the worst in people? – insecurity, micromanagement, internal politics and misaligned ambition.

More than a decade ago, taking a walk in a park, one of us saw an interesting (and all too rare) sign: "Please Walk on the Grass". Quite a surprise – and difference – from the normal "Don't" instruction; a tangible reminder of the essence of what good leadership is all about – the art of unlocking and exploiting the 'can do'. People can be like rubber bands – they have this wonderful capacity for stretch – if only we provide the pull, and the opportunities. Leadership – at all levels, *and* upwards and sideways, as well as 'downwards' – is all about creating an environment where people can be the best they can possibly be.

> *Inspirational leadership empowers people. It gets them excited and passionate about their work.*

> *My job as a leader is to ignite and sustain the passion of others – and figure out how to do that in a professional situation where lots of the people are introverted to some degree.*

In pursuit of excellence…

> *The key thing about herding cats successfully is to have top quality cats.*

Having good people is *the* important step to operational success in an organisation, closely followed by delivering the goals you have set to the highest standard you can, across all aspects of the business you are in. So, on your team, you need to have the best people you can find:

> "The people with the best people win." Jerry Welch (1948-) Innovative marketing executive.

> *We target the best people around the world and then make it easy and attractive for them to spend time with us.*

> *Recruit the best and make it clear that excellence is the prime requirement.*

There was, quite a while back, a radio interview with management expert and author Charles Handy, in which he talked about strategy and success. He told of a discussion with a senior school headmaster, reported to be 'the best of the best'. This man's secret, evidently, was along the lines of "It's easy. All I did was appoint the best Heads of Houses, and the best Heads of Department I could find, and then got out of the way. And waited five years."

It's not always quite that easy – (just) hiring 'good people and letting them do whatever they want' is certainly no guarantee of success and may indeed lead to real problems. Handy, rightly, went on to talk about the overarching importance of a sound 'framing' strategy (see Section 11) where good people can excel. Getting the culture, systems and organisation environment right are also important. But there's real wisdom in the headmaster's observation about the criticality of good people.

How do we know what – or, rather, who – is good? The answer does not come without endeavour; thus, it is absolutely necessary to do your homework and observe. Firstly, track record is always a pretty sound indicator of (projected) future performance. Secondly, make sure you access, first hand reports – down, up and sideways – not just formal referees' reports from former 'bosses' or supervisors, but also perspectives from well-respected peers, colleagues, subordinates, students. Thirdly, ask yourself: is this person an enthusiastic spirit? And – importantly – can he or she ignite that enthusiasm in others? Finally, are there clear signs that the goals you seek are going to be delivered? Some intelligent, articulate, passionate enthusiasts are closet non-deliverers – which a careful assessment of track record, sometimes 'reading between the lines' of written or verbal feedback, will hopefully (but, regrettably, not always) uncover.

> *'Talent attracts talent.' Get an outstanding individual on board, in a particular area, and other high achievers will join, seeking the chance to work with (or continue working with) the 'star'.*

> *People come – and stay – here because they can work with the brightest people in the world on important problems.*

The secret of success?... In order to foster success and achieve excellence it is critical to be aware of the underlying elements that are essential in reaching those goals. Many argue very persuasively that personal drive and single-mindedness are critical characteristics.

> "The average person puts only 25 percent of his energy and ability into his work. The world takes off its hat to those who put in more than 50 percent of their capacity, and stands on its head for those few and far between souls who devote 100 percent." Andrew Carnegie (1835-1919) US industrialist and philanthropist.

Finding and keeping the passion is the biggest role you can play as a leader.

> "The real secret of success is enthusiasm. You can do anything if you have enthusiasm. Enthusiasm is the yeast that makes your hope rise to the stars. Enthusiasm is the sparkle in your eye, it is the swing in your gait, the grip of your hand, the irresistible surge of your will and your energy to execute your ideas. Enthusiasts are fighters. They have fortitude, they have staying qualities. Enthusiasm is at the bottom of all progress. With it there is accomplishment. Without it there are only alibis." Walter Chrysler (1875-1940) American automotive industry executive.

The worlds of academia and research are replete with examples of intelligently applied enthusiasm and focused drive overcoming great obstacles.

> "The key is to keep company only with people who uplift you, whose presence calls forth your best." Chad Harbach (*The Art of Fielding*, 2012)

Moving up... When strong performers consistently produce quality outputs, it is necessary for that to be recognised. One natural form of recognition is advancement in the organisation. The skills needed in delivery are often those needed in leading and managing – the producers of today are the leaders of tomorrow. If this is you, here's some advice:

If you trust the people you are working for, stay. If not, leave... If trust is positive both up and down, then be patient... because your superiors will want you to continue to be successful... and so you must wait until the right opportunity arises to move you up to a position of more responsibility that you can handle and become an evident (and so promotable) success.

Be brave... say "Yes" to new challenges. If your boss has hopes for you, he or she will want to prepare you for later promotions. In my case, my immediate boss once asked me if I knew anything about biology. I said "No". So he said "In that case you had better run the Biology Department" (which, at that time, was headed up by an internationally famous expert in photosynthesis who had just been elected to the National Academy of Sciences).

Broaden your interests. The field in which you first established your reputation is not the only field of interest in the world. Spend time (like lunch breaks) with experts in other fields of science. As a young materials scientist, I developed a real competitive edge through my conversations with brilliant organic and physical chemists... for example, learning that there are other solvents in the world besides water.

Noting also from these last two recommendations – as we recounted in Section 3 (on Collaboration) – getting skilled as a 'boundary crosser' can have real benefits in advancing your career.

Selecting people... Next to getting the strategy right, this is probably the most important thing you will need to master as a leader.

I would have valued knowing both how hard it is to hire the right person for the job and how critical it is to make the correct match. If you hire right, management is easier.

We are very careful in hiring new people. Thereafter our leadership role is to help them to be successful. We work very hard on this. If they don't make it, we feel disappointed.

The average staff member's career with us is about eleven years. Which means, when you're making an appointment, you are – on average – making a million-dollar decision, and that's the direct salary cost only. Compare and contrast the time and effort put into other million-dollar decisions (like equipment acquisition) and you'll find many appointment processes are seriously underdone.

Getting a good 'hit rate' in making staff appointments is imperative. And getting a variety of different inputs and perspectives: internally – more senior, peer and more junior – as well as those from external people, can be very valuable in helping you make the decision.

There's a great moment in the film *Dead Poets Society* where the schoolteacher (played by Robin Williams), jumps up onto a desk and makes a point to his class about the importance of getting a different perspective: "Up here, I look different to you; down there, you look different to me." Thus, engaging a variety of people in the selection process can provide valuable insight, including about those people themselves. This can all be time-consuming, but almost invariably it is well worth the effort.

For senior appointments we ran three (advisory to me) selection committees, each interviewing all shortlisted candidates – bosses plus some peers; subordinates; and (external) stakeholders. Rarely did they reach the same conclusion. But the wealth of insight and differing perspectives greatly improved the chances of getting the decision right.

By running appointment committees myself, not only am I in charge of a critical appointment, but I learn a lot about the people on the committee.

Be very clear about who owns the appointment: committee(s) don't; ownership is your responsibility. On those occasions when an appointment doesn't work out, people will run for cover.

> *I've never used a truly democratic process for finally appointing members of my immediate team. I'm the one on the line, since I have to work with them on a day-to-day basis. And I'm responsible for the results we achieve.*

And, as mentioned above, the real support and mentoring work starts the day the new member of staff accepts the job.

Two important 'last words' in the selection/hiring game:

One – no matter what the urgency, it is always better not to appoint than to appoint the wrong person. Often this means resisting pressure from others who see (and frequently exaggerate) the problems associated with delay.

In any appointment process, it is, of course, necessary to ensure that it is fully justifiable in terms of openness and transparency, and with respect to your institution's goals of diversity and equal opportunity. But ....

> *Always make the best appointment – not the 'almost best' because of other influences or pressures.*

Two – when hiring in the academic and research worlds, you're frequently in the long-term building of relationships. For example:

> *When you take on a new research student, very often you're taking on a relationship for life.*

Personal relationships are vital in all that we do, and can be revisited with interest a surprising amount of time later.

On stretch… People have great capacity for demanding tasks - stretch. And this can – and should – be cascaded 'down' through each level in the organisation.

> *I once played a game, at Christmas time, with my senior leadership group. They could either come with me to a Bach organ recital, or they could craft a patentable invention in their area of expertise before the holiday break. Well, would you believe it – several succeeded in developing the basis for some valuable patents we subsequently took out.*

When you stretch your people and tell them that they are capable of doing far more than they think they can, they do perform and indeed can outperform their own concept of themselves.

There's no doubt that encouragement and persuasion work best. But people don't just need praise, they need to believe that you think that they have the skills to do even better.

Qualification(s)… Three points here. One – qualifications are a guide not a rule book. Two – 'credentials' go way beyond the paper qualifications. Three – due diligence pays. Always double check that you're getting what you think you're getting. Competition for jobs can do funny things to people, particularly in hard times. There are, sadly, far too many examples of appointments being based on misinformation.

The diversity challenge, and the 'affirmative action' paradox…

It is the responsibility of the leader to encourage diversity …. This is more than just encouraging women and ethnic minorities to enter higher education but also encouraging them to apply for posts and promotions, as well as facilitating their progress into jobs, such as by working with schools, offering 'apprenticeships', and mentoring schemes once they've joined.

There is, necessarily, significant emphasis on equal opportunities and related legislation in the prevailing employment climate. This means that great care must be given to ensuring that all the procedures up to any final selection meet the required standards. But this can occasionally allow paradoxical issues to surface. When does a manifest commitment to equality of opportunity become 'affirmative action'? In many jurisdictions the former is a legal requirement, the latter is not. It is important that this difference is both recognised and understood.

Yet…

It was amazing to see how the diversity in our leadership team improved the richness of our discussions, and the quality of our decision taking.

We just weren't getting female applicants for our post-doctoral fellowships. Evidently they thought they wouldn't stand much chance. So we ran a 'women only' round, weathered the outrage, and got a really good number of quality applications. We made three outstanding appointments, who are all doing splendidly.

At the end of the day, the lifeblood of all committed organisations is ideas, and…

"Where do new ideas come from? That's simple. From differences. The best way to maximise differences is to mix ages, cultures, disciplines. Hire diversity." Nicholas Negroponte (1943-) American architect and founder of the MIT Media Lab.

Negroponte's suggestion to 'hire diversity' is apt, but we would extend it. We would suggest that the appointment process should endeavour to meet, in addition, as wide a range of diversity as possible. Subject to the specific requirements of the job, this would include ensuring in one's team a range of diversity in race, gender, ethnicity, social and educational background, and life experience.

There is no doubt that a more evenly balanced leadership team is an attraction for talent.

The business case for more diverse appointments was clear – we were losing talent. No quick fix, but more role models appointed and getting the 'pipeline' (supply-side) flowing has got us moving.

New brooms versus old brooms?… Often there are very good reasons for bringing in a 'new broom'. But most organisations of our type are brimming with talent, people you know, ready to take on new challenges and opportunities. And, of course, they will have a pretty good idea of what they're letting themselves in for.

"I use the rule of 50 per cent. Try to find somebody inside your organisation with a record of success and an appetite for the job. If he or she looks like 50 per cent of what you need, give them the job. In six months they'll have grown the other 50 per cent – and everybody will be satisfied." Robert Townsend (1920-1998) President and CEO of Avis.

On judgement... Along with enthusiasm and track record, sound judgement can be a most important attribute in choosing and promoting staff.

When it comes to people, if there's one key word it's 'judgement' – the ability to assess the situation, give the best advice and take the best course of action.

Here, as in making quality decisions (see Section 4), intuition plays a part. Judgement is not something that can be taught. If it is to be learned at all, it is learned through observation and experience. Once gained, it is a great asset.

To lead successfully you need to have developed a track record such that people trust your judgement.

Another paradox here is illustrated through the old story around making quality judgements: "Q: How do you make good decisions? A: Through experience. Q: But how do you get experience? A: Through making bad decisions."

You can teach the detailed technical leadership, but you can't teach the bigger picture stuff; it's an experience thing. Some have this ability, and some find it difficult.

Building the team... The necessity is to harness both individualism *and* the strength of the team:

"Many of the best ideas, concepts, prototypes and innovations come from a single person's insight. You get these amazing bits of work from inspired individuals who have the freedom to act, when they have the tools and knowledge they need. But to scale any operation takes the work of teams, and, more often than not, teams of teams. Leaders inspire that flash of genius and also make those individuals want to work together. Great teamwork is a real skill. Finding a way to nurture individual passion and pride while at the same time creating a spirit of teamwork is a hallmark of the leaders I admire most. Pulling off both of those in the same organization is magical but essential." Mark Shuttleworth (1973-) IT entrepreneur and the world's second self-funded space tourist.

The role of leaders… in a global world is now almost too big and difficult for any one individual. We look for heroes, but true leadership is now in teams.

There is a lot of very good information available about teams, and about the demands of building them and leading them effectively. There are also useful tools, such as the Myers-Briggs Type Indicator and the Belbin Team Role Inventory, for gaining better understanding of individuals and of how they see their roles in teams.

Never underestimate the power of positive camaraderie in the senior leadership team. When they all believe in the vision and mission and strategy, the people hear the same message, although it may be expressed differently.

I gained a lot by using a consultant to find out what I needed to know about teams and their collective merits.

Carefully planned, and very carefully managed, 'team building' sessions can also be useful when designed to complement 'on the job' learning. Five-star, objective, facilitation is fundamentally important – a 'make or break' imperative. Here your detailed spadework in facilitator selection is the order of the day.

For transformation you often need first to transform the management team.

I underestimated how long it would it would take to change the culture of the senior management group towards my way of working, and away from that of my predecessor.

But in making the transformations it is important to avoid setting up, deliberately or inadvertently, what might be seen as an 'inner' group:

> *Beware the 'Kitchen Cabinet'. Don't have an A-team and a B-team. You usually have some very good people who deliver quality, quickly; and others less so. But always favouring A-players with tough, stretching assignments builds up the pressure on them, and resentment of those they see not working so hard. Resentment on both sides, in fact, as the B-players may well feel that they are regarded as 'outsiders'. Your leadership job is also to build the skills of the B-players on your team.*

The time and effort you spend with and developing your team needs to be appropriately balanced with the quality, one-on-one time spent with your individual team members – and all done of course in the context of the objectives you are seeking to achieve. Simply put, it is all about the 'three-legged stool' balancing act of leadership: task-team-individual.

> *Too often, especially under pressure, the whole focus is on getting the job done, 'whatever it takes'. Regrettably, when we are not careful, 'it' can detract from the team-building and individual-growing responsibilities which are key to balanced leadership.*

Then 'task' has become all, and it's like a stool with only one, fat, long leg – unstable, and not sustainable.

Developing the talent... Visible and tangible commitment from, and engagement with, top management is a key to the success of leadership development programmes – helping colleagues develop their skills both in their current roles and in preparation for roles to come. If the processes are simply routine activities, run by the Human Resources department, then a lack of commitment is more than likely. Certainly this should be a top priority for the leader.

> *Leadership development is critical for our future. We need to put in substantially more effort here. It's probably the chief executive's only sustainable legacy.*

If I had my time again I would devote three times as much time and resource to nurturing our leadership development programs.

The most important test of a successful leader is, in my view, the extent to which he or she has contributed to the development of the leadership capability of others across many levels within the institution.

As leaders we are in the people-growing business. There's a Chinese proverb which states: "If you want a year of wealth, grow grain; if you want ten years of wealth, grow trees; if you want a hundred years of wealth, grow people."

"The conductor doesn't make a sound. The conductor's power depends on his ability to make other people powerful." Benjamin Zander (1939-) formerly Conductor and Music Director of the Boston Philharmonic Youth Orchestra.

Caring for the talent (and everybody else)... There are also other, more domestic, aspects of dealing with your staff that should not be overlooked. More is required than just giving attention to the mechanics of management. As we have noted previously, good leaders and managers also have a human face, which can show in a variety of ways – such as concern about matters outside the workplace or an awareness of important health or family issues. Of course, this must be tempered by taking care about possible intrusion on privacy. Experience shows that different people respond to different overtures in different ways. Nevertheless, there is merit in making it clear that there is a sense of caring within the organisation.

Strongly promoting workplace safety and health – even 'bike to work' programmes, or 'fruit and nuts not biscuits' at tea-times – says we care about your health in your place of work and, therefore, we care about you.

And that includes non-academic support staff... While an army (reportedly) marches on its stomach – and your 'soldiers' (academics and researchers) are the front-liners – all academic and research organisations are operationally very dependent on the quality and efficiency of their 'support' staff – even though they don't necessarily always realise it. The care and attention given to senior staff and colleagues must be balanced by an awareness of the needs of others in the organisation since they are also prominent ambassadors 'around town', and a litmus test for organisational health.

> *It's good to stay in touch with the janitors and technical and support staff. They usually know a lot more about what's going on and where the issues and problems are than your senior staff do.*

'Signs and symbols' – of inclusivity and equality – are often closely examined as indicators of a leader's commitment (or otherwise) to parity of esteem and opportunity:

> *I tried always to find ways to make it very clear that our support and technical staff were very important – joint common rooms – visibility and senior level representation on promotions committees – and even down to equality of car parking – the latter not without some contention, I might add!*

And on the topic of incentives and motivation… This can be a difficult area. There are many different ways that people respond to incentives, and, therefore, many alternatives in providing incentives. It is necessary to think (significantly) beyond simple financial rewards:

> *It is important to try to understand what motivates people. Our type of environment is very different from 'normal' business life, and you can't work it out in one meeting. And the motivators can be very different – personal (financial) reward is rarely the driver. For example… Prof A is a great host, facilitates workshops and conferences, and makes people welcome – he has built a global family and keeping it in touch and harmonious is his prime driver. Dr B has put personal fellowship money into her research group to support her team and the working environment she has created. Personal prestige is Prof C's key motivator – the awards she gets, the media*

appearances – it is all about recognition, and looking good. Dr D, the easiest to deal with, is motivated by remuneration (and, in particular, how he is doing relative to others). Prof E – a bit like Dr B – is motivated by seeing his staff and students do well – he enjoys being 'the shoulders for them to climb on'. Drs F and G are solely and obsessively motivated by the intellectual challenge and the problem, the research question they are seeking to answer."

In the motivation stakes, in a cats culture, titles can be important:

Even though they all say they don't respect hierarchy, they enjoy being called 'Dr' or 'Professor' – and the label on their door can mean a lot to them.

If you know what the primary personal drivers are, you can better craft the incentive structures to support optimal performance.

What motivates people? Recognition. And time, and freedom – giving them the space where they can take the credit…

Opportunities and encouragement to innovate bring out the best in people. The ability to fly with something that catches their eye will keep cats happy and energised.

The management of creative professionals starts and ends with encouraging, supporting and incentivising achievement.

But about remuneration… The pay cheque, we are often told, is a second-order priority for individuals who choose a career in academia or research. This may be so, but it is an increasingly important competitive component in the talent attraction and retention stakes. And too important for you not to be reasonably hands-on in the process of setting salaries. We are not (yet) into professional footballer type trading, but top talent can certainly negotiate hard.

And while, in an ideal, fully transparent world, it might seem entirely reasonable that everyone should know exactly what everyone else is earning, confidentiality considerations and restrictions generally make this a hard thing to do in practice. And human nature being what it is, the 'workers in the vineyard' parable (Matthew 20: 1-16) would undoubtedly apply – people previously 'happy' with their pay could become instantly unhappy when they see, without any explanation, what some others are getting. Suffice it to say that, in any decision-making situation, you should be able, if called upon to do so, to justify each and every decision, hand on heart, and communicate honestly and transparently.

Managing performance…

You need to be honest with people. Straight with them. Sometimes it's very hard. Good people welcome an honest appraisal of how they're doing.

Whenever I mentor a new manager and potential leader my number one piece of advice is 'be as honest as possible'… Trust builds a strong team and is essential for them to believe in that vision.

Dr Rod Eddington, a former CEO of British Airways, tells of a defining intervention in his career when he was Deputy CEO of Cathay Pacific Airways. They enhanced skills across the whole organisation in giving and receiving the day-to-day feedback essential to holding people accountable and managing for good performance. While 'feedback is the food of champions' – it is how we all improve and grow – giving feedback is often hard to do, and even harder to do well. Get some coaching, experiment through role-playing – practice and more practice. It is a never-ending journey.

I would have benefited from more strategic leadership and mentoring on performance management right from the start.

Universities and research organisations which draw on specialist expertise are often not very good at performance management, and the more senior the

> *member of staff, the harder it is to deal with underperformance.*

Getting off on the right foot, like the 'catch them doing things right' advice we were given while raising our children is all important...

> *Before getting to what you want achieved, start with praise and not what's wrong with the current arrangements. If you start with what's wrong, usually people don't hear the way forward.*

There's a story, noted by Marcus Buckingham and Ashley Goodall in their 2019 *Harvard Business Review* article, about how Tom Landry, the legendary coach of the Dallas Cowboys, turned around his struggling team. While the other teams were reviewing missed tackles and dropped balls, Landry instead combed through footage of previous games and created, for each player, a highlight reel of when the player had done something easily, naturally and effectively. Landry reasoned that while the number of wrong ways to do something was infinite, the number of right ways, for any particular player, was not. It was knowable, and the best way to discover it was to look at plays where that person had done it excellently. From now on, he told each team member, "we only replay your winning plays".

Now on one level he was doing this to make his team members feel better about themselves because he knew the power of praise. But according to the story, Landry wasn't nearly as interested in praise as he was in learning. His instincts told him that each person would improve his performance most if he could see, in slow motion, what his own personal version of excellence looked like.

You can do the same. Whenever you see one of your people do something that worked for you, that rocked your world just a little, stop for a minute and highlight it. By helping your team member recognise what excellence looks like – by saying, "That! Yes, that!" – you are offering the chance to gain an insight; you are highlighting a pattern that is already there within them so that they can recognise it, anchor it, re-create it, and refine it. That is learning.

Getting really good at managing performance is without doubt a skill worth acquiring:

> *Around feedback, one great boss I had was a genius. I would go in for a chat, get a clear message where improvement was needed, but come out feeling good about myself and about our relationship, and fired up.*

> *With good leaders people learn. They create the playing field for success.*

> *The best bosses I've had help you see something in yourself you haven't seen. They are adaptive to different styles and create the dialogue that allows learning to occur, and they empower their people to make choices, and to grow, providing a safety net to do so. You walk out with insight, not feeling beaten up.*

Overall, therefore, it is the day-to-day assessments that are key, and necessary for the good manager's armoury. But 'formal' performance appraisals (e.g. yearly) often can have questionable value, especially as they can make an artificial short-term event out of a continuing responsibility. And at the end of the day, again...

> *What do I look for from my boss? Consistency and honesty – both when I've done well and when I've messed up.*

Organising the team... Structure is the servant of talent management and strategy – not vice versa. But there is a paradox here. On the one hand, deciding 'who you want on your bus' is a priority. Flexible structures (and titles) can facilitate the recruitment, and the retention, of talented performers, and should be used as such. You need to take into account the potential unintended consequences and perceived precedent-settings that may arise. Conversely, compromising your own organisational design principles (and probably confusing the rest of your organisation) to move individuals sideways rather than moving them 'out' is invariably a mistake.

Letting them go: the trials and tribulations of termination…
This is an area of activity that more often than not makes people uncomfortable. But it is part of the territory of leading and managing. It is certain that, as a new leader, you will, surprisingly early in your tenure, encounter a situation where one of the team you have inherited (or even someone you yourself have hired) is either identified as not having the skills expected or just does not fit in with the new ethos. And they may have to go.

I wish, in my earlier career, that I'd spent more time learning about leadership which might have mitigated my two biggest management faults: lack of clarity about where I wanted to take the organisation, and lack of decisiveness in dispensing with inadequate people.

Most often, here, we are not talking about issues of gross incompetence, financial irregularity or inappropriate behaviour, but a simple manifestation of the 'Peter Principle' which states that "a person who is competent at their job can earn promotion to a position which may well require different skills. If he or she lacks the skills required for the new role, or cannot quickly attain them, they will be incompetent at the new level, and will likely not be promoted again. If, however, the person is competent in the new role, they may be promoted again, and could continue to be promoted until reaching a level at which they are incompetent. Being incompetent, the individual will not qualify for promotion again, and so will remain stuck at this final level."

So, the sooner you realise that 'this isn't working' the better. Again this is a place to trust your intuition in taking the first steps. And determining an effective way forward is then the order of the day. Providing timely, honest, unambiguous feedback is critical – delayed, mixed messages just muddy the water:

You're not doing anyone a favour by keeping him or her on in a job they're not up to. It's not kind to be kind – it's cruel to be kind.

Re-defining or re-scoping the non-achiever's job, for example by reducing their span of responsibility, can work on some occasions, particularly where you yourself have been responsible for creating a 'mission impossible' job, or have perhaps overestimated a person's strengths and talents. But this is not often the best solution.

It is hard getting rid of people, and I've never been very good at it.

Letting a colleague go is hard, and can be more painful than it needs to be. Rarely will your task be made easier by the person involved 'falling on their sword'. Also, because all action must conform with the legal frameworks within which the organisation operates, leaders may worry about legal comebacks, get officious and behave insensitively or even abnormally. 'Do as you would be done by' is a good guideline:

In the commercial world there is greater emphasis on being successful, and somewhat less on being compassionate. In our world you need to be sure to emphasise both.

So your target should be one of seeking to help the individual, using care and investing time and support – and generosity (not necessarily financial generosity) – in identifying separation possibilities, including the prospect of moving on to a next assignment, probably outside the organisation. More often than not the individual concerned ends up happier too (though maybe not in the first instance).

I have often been surprised by how many 'failing' colleagues have known deep down that they are proverbial square pegs in round holes.

The trick is to find a way, as far as possible, to help a colleague save face and maintain his or her self-esteem without inadvertently compromising your own values or credibility or business objectives. How, when, and what you – together – communicate therefore makes a huge difference.

In the challenge of termination, there are also two notable 'Bewares':

Number 1: The Two-Year Rule

> *Over a twenty-year period we observed that it was typically two years (at least) from when we (or I) first observed 'smoke under the door' to the point when the person concerned left that job, or the organisation.*

> *Deferring a decision because "He's only got 18 months to run on his contract" can be a mistake. A lot of damage can be done in 18 months.*

Number 2: "But They're So Difficult"

> *You can't fire people for being difficult. Most organisations have their share of very clever, single minded, and often rather difficult people, but our type of organisation is often stacked with them. I've seen difficult (but clever and competent) people be a 'burr under the saddle' for a decade. You have to accept it and manage around them.*

Perversely, of course, it is also important to remember that 'difficult people' are often the source of some of your success:

> *An academic's job is to ask why. And they certainly ask questions.*

> "Business needs a massive transfusion of talent; and talent, I believe, is most likely to be found among non-conformists, dissenters and rebels." David Ogilvy (1911-1999) British advertising executive.

An intractable challenge… Finally, one of the most intractable challenges in the 'cats' environment is re-motivating, or moving out, the borderline performer:

> *This is one of the toughest problems we have. I struggle with the 'coasters': they're not terrible. But they'll write one paper a year, not three. And they have one graduate student, not three or four. I have no good answers here. You just have to get more Machiavellian.*

But maybe they are just being measured by the wrong yardstick. For example, their research record (and interest) has gone seriously off the boil, but they may be great teachers, or exceedingly efficient administrators. Changing the goalposts – if you can – could then be a quick and effective fix. You can give them time off, and away, to re-invent themselves (and, perhaps, to look for a job elsewhere). You can bite the bullet, and buy them out – although this is usually good only as a last resort, unless there is real urgency. And you can have (time-consuming, and usually frustrating) 'deep and meaningful' dialogues, to seek to identify a mutually beneficial way forward. But all in all, termination is never easy and never without pain.

On the brighter side, through such processes – and with the benefit of hindsight – there should be opportunities for improving your hiring and tenure practices.

Disciplinary action… This is best avoided, if you can avoid it – without compromising your principles, or those of the organisation. It is a last resort, and there are no winners. The only real exception is when the law has been broken – then it is necessary to act quickly and firmly, making it very clear to all that there are forms of behaviour which are totally unacceptable. Proven corruption, harassment and theft come to mind. But, aside from ensuring procedural fairness, as we emphasise in Section 9, paying very careful attention to communication processes in such cases is essential.

A final reminder (and lest we forget)…

All business is people business. Full stop.

9. COMMUNICATION, COMMUNICATION, COMMUNICATION

No matter how hard you try, the most consistent complaint will be about poor communication... you should accept the criticism and try harder still... never stop trying to communicate better.

Communication? We never do enough.

Again, consistently strong communication clearly and regularly, remains so important with all the ambiguity, noise and fake news around. Including 'up' – 'no surprises management' remains critical.

John O'Neil, who runs the Center for Leadership Renewal in San Francisco calls communications excellence 'the baton of leadership'. We agree and offer elaboration in the following sections.

A daily problem... If you look, objectively, at the disasters (big or small) that you've observed in the past, both in your organisation and elsewhere, a high percentage might be laid – in part or in whole – at the door of inter-person communication problems.

There is the well-known – but perhaps not sufficiently taken to heart – World War I story: the major and his troops are in the trenches, up to their ears in mud and blood, wanting to move. Communications are down; he sends a message "Send reinforcements, we're going to advance." A couple of miles back, with the verbal message having been passed on a couple of times, the general in charge hears "Send three and fourpence; we're going to a dance." How often have you seen this kind of miscommunication?

Not communicating clearly... brings out the worst in people.

He may have had good reasons for what he did, but these were not perceived by those expected to work with the results. Uncommunicated intentions mean very little.

Person-to-person and person-to-people communication stuff-ups cost our organisation heaps in terms of lost time, unnecessary re-work, demotivation and upset. Ah – if I had but one wish from someone with a magic wand…!

Communication and change… Much leadership time is taken up in the effective management of change. Reflecting on studies by Prosci USA, major consultants in change management, of many organisations in states of change, effective and otherwise, it is clear that well-conducted and well-managed communication is a dominant factor in successfully implementing change.

If you have a vision and you expect your people to run with it, but they don't properly understand it, you're probably going to fail.

"Stop nuancing. Simple, clear messages get through." John McTernan (formerly Director of Political Operations for UK Prime Minister, Tony Blair, and Communications Director for Australian Prime Minister, Julia Gillard).

In any change process, you need to be crystal clear – in your own mind, to your team, and to the organisation – about the direction in which you're headed:

You must, repeat must, keep your strategic messages very clear: very straightforward, easily understood and digestible – simple terms, easy to remember and to understand, and to pass on. And then repeat, repeat, repeat. Be boring.

Sometimes you seem to need to repeat things at least seven times and then people begin to understand!

Listening skills… Communication is two-way and, as author Stephen Covey wisely observed, "Seek first to understand, then to be understood".

Most leaders talk too much... it's an occupational hazard.

Even in a senior and sophisticated management group you can never assume that what is being heard by a set of ears is that which comes out of a particular mouth.

You need to develop ways to check that your communication is effective. Do not assume it is and do not assume repetition will make it more so. Listening to something meaningful can be a strength of 'cats' – hearing is not the same thing.

You know when they are really listening, as opposed to thinking about the next point they want to make. Good leaders help people in active listening – to be both emotionally as well as physically present.

For you as a leader, the old maxim, previously mentioned, that 'feedback is the food of champions' definitely applies. Indeed, you should be going out of your way – and role modelling – to make it easy and non-threatening for your colleagues to comment when they see you falling short.

It's imperative to listen to criticisms from the team and really pay attention. It takes guts to tell a senior executive they are making mistakes, and if only a couple tell you then probably lots of others are thinking the same.

We have robust conversations in a respectful way. We track the outcomes of those conversations, and then operationalise them.

It was tough moving into a leadership position where virtually everybody was older than me. Some, a lot so. I quickly learned to watch my words, listen, learn from them.

But regrettably...

Sometimes, extremely capable leaders just stop listening. They get weak people around them and get stuck, and become enamoured with their own ability. Eventually they self-destruct.

The personal touch…

The more you can achieve personal contact, with frank and honest communication, the better.

People want to know what's going on, and want to hear it directly from the leader. Even if they don't like what they hear.

Adults like stories, just as children like stories. Especially those stories with a personal, experiential flavour:

Stories are very important in communication.

Stories provide an emotional resonance. Better still if they've got a rational, analytic base.

Be creative… Colleagues from Xerox tell the (apocryphal?) story of staff complaining in the common way about senior management: "They never tell us what's going on around here", while noting that if a juicy rumour is put into the organisation, in twenty minutes everybody knows all about it! Evidently they changed their communication processes to mirror more closely the way in which rumours get conveyed – with considerable positive benefit.

If you think your message 'from the top' will be 'cascaded' accurately, timeously (or even at all), think again – get real, and creative.

Whether it's good news or bad, we always try to ensure that our staff members know it first, and don't first read about it in the newspapers or on the internet.

Actions versus words…

I communicate behaviours every day. Sometimes I even use words.

Words are only a small percentage of the message. An illustrative anecdote: the gifted communicator, Nelson Mandela, preached reconciliation in creating a new South Africa from the schisms of apartheid. He also lived his words… he knew that the game of rugby football and the

South African representative team, the Springboks, had dominated the white man's sporting agenda in that nation. At the 1995 Rugby World Cup Final in Johannesburg, President Mandela came onto the ground to meet the teams wearing a Number 6 Springbok rugby football jersey (a replica of that of the Springbok captain, François Pienaar). No words were spoken that the crowd could hear, but the very largely white audience in the stadium got the message, loud and clear – the new South Africa was going to be about reconciliation, sharing and teamwork. Many present had tears in their eyes. Actions can speak louder than words, so they say.

Relatedly, and in contrast, there's the old saying along the lines of "I can't hear what you're saying, because it is drowned out by what I see you doing."

If you are pronouncing values for your organisation, and at the same time you show your own behaviour is inconsistent and you are doing things that don't respect these values, you only fail once.

Summarising 'the story so far'… Communication issues often lead to (twice? thrice?) daily problems. 'Getting it right' – key to managing any successful change initiative (see also Section 12) – requires honing your listening skills (as opposed to your talking skills, which you probably do pretty well). It is very much enhanced by the personal touch and often requires creativity and imagination. What you do (as opposed to what you say) also generally communicates volumes.

We now move on, in this communication-related section, to some other thorny communication-related issues such as email, the media (social and otherwise), PowerPoint and annual reports.

Beware the tyranny of the email…

I was told that there are now close to 300 billion emails sent every day. That's 2.8 million every second. Or approximately 90 trillion each year. Happily some 80 per cent go straight to junk mail. Half of the rest seem to end up in my inbox.

The rise and rise of email is both a blessing and a potential problem. Instead of being a valuable aid to communication, emails can become both a consuming tyranny and a landscape fraught with danger. It is quite normal for the common courtesies of letters to be cast to the winds – especially in a 'cats' environment, since many 'cats' can be quite cantankerous. It is surprising just how many times you see statements in emails that are ill-judged and intemperate in ways that were rare in old-fashioned correspondence.

Emails seem to engender a sense of urgency that can become quite out of proportion:

When my prime objective became clearing my inbox each day, I knew I had my priorities quite wrong.

There is no difficult email (or letter) which cannot be improved by eight hours sleep.

On email, nobody ever has the last word.

If you are not careful, your words can also be used – selectively, and out of context – against you.

Our environments tend to be pretty leaky. I ended up never crafting an email (except to my team, or other close colleagues, etc.) without thinking through how it (or an extract) would come across on the front page of the local newspaper, or in a parliamentary committee.

If you're communicating something important by email, never assume that it has been read, and understood. "But I sent you an email!" is a very lame excuse.

There is still a place for the old-fashioned letter… A golden rule – when you've got something nice to say, write a letter; where there's a problem, pick up the phone or, better still, if you can, go across for a chat. It is amazing how often people get this the wrong way round. Thus:

> *Communicating in writing when a face-to-face meeting is required usually brings out the worst in people.*

Both in you and in them.

Mass messaging… To many, email is not communication – it is broadcasting. Whether or not your mass email messages have been seen, understood and internalised is often very open to question.

> *'Global' emails (to all staff) are not often viewed positively by staff as a method of communication – too top-down, too impersonal, the voice 'from the top of the mountain'.*

> *As one of my top industry friends says, it's so nice and easy to send twenty thousand emails by pressing one button, but I've not yet worked out how to answer them all.*

To be realistic, however, when large numbers of staff need to be communicated with quickly and efficiently, email is a boon. Thus, judicious and creative use of email can provide a solid means of information transfer and of keeping people in the picture. But these messages must usually be simple, short and clear. Draft them, and test them by seeking feedback on them from a colleague whose judgement you trust. Try hard to avoid typos – "Even the boss isn't into quality, so why should *I* bother?"

Reply to your emails…

> *If you want them to be receptive, you need to be responsive.*

> *What brings out the best in people? Engage with them. Respond to every email.*

Maybe we're well into stating the obvious, but it's usually a good idea to try to deal with your emails personally (and promptly), rather than have them vetted for you – important messages can get missed. This doesn't mean you need to draft all the responses. It can be very efficient to look your emails over and then forward them (probably with brief comments) to be handled, personally and timeously, by someone close to you whose judgement and finesse you value.

A simple but valuable stratagem for allaying the fears of colleagues that they are being ignored or overlooked, is to generate very basic responses along the lines of "Thank you for your message. I will get back to you shortly/by this afternoon/tomorrow/next week" – and then make sure that you *do* that! This quick-shot reply can help to bring the temperature down and keep relationships intact.

> *With 300+ emails a day, I needed some prioritisation system. What works for me is automatic sorting to give me #1: from outside, addressed to me; #2: from inside addressed to me; #3: all emails addressed to me but as one of a number of recipients; #4: all where I'm just copied in, Cc or Bcc.*

> *Blind copying can be a problem. As well as clogging up my inbox, what do I do with information I'm not supposed to have, apart from worry about it? A colleague banned all blind copying in his organisation, evidently to good effect.*

Social media... Over the ten years since our original *Herding Cats* book, it is probably not an overstatement to refer to the 'explosion' of social media. Everywhere we are surrounded by Twitter, Facebook, LinkedIn, Instagram, YouTube and a good deal more – it's very much part of our landscape.

And they can have both positive and negative features, which lead to some quite different, polarised – and polarising - views, for example...

> *I loathe it. I despise it. It can be an echo chamber where people can project by anonymity to do their worst. In my view the explosion of social media has helped lead to a lot of the angst and divisiveness that we see flying around amongst our communities.*

When I was running a high-profile program I religiously followed social media every day. It was ugly. It was too emotionally confronting. You have to protect yourself. I now haven't looked at it for years.

Sadly, social media is all too often where extreme views are expressed, usually in opposition to something, and strong opposition at that. It is not a good guide as to how the community at large feels. It is also generally not a good litmus test for actual performance.

How do we respond collectively to an environment where what's 'right' isn't determined by the law but by what's on Twitter?

On the other hand …

I love social media, it has allowed me to network and meet incredible professionals and communicators across the world. In many cases, a connection on Twitter or LinkedIn has turned into a long-term collaborator. I always check out social media activity before hiring too, it is a great way to get a feel for someone's authenticity.

Social media may bring big challenges – but it's also a wonderful feedback and promotional tool and can be used very effectively as such.

Social media allows you to get in front of all types of people as we all carry around a smartphone or device these days and choose which news we want to see. Thus, used the right way, it allows us to call out behaviours, to directly challenge fake news and present an expert view on particular issues.

The use of social media needs to be managed…

"These (social media platforms) are the new operating systems for the 21st-century enterprise in the sense that these are the platforms upon which talent works, and performs, and creates capability." Don Tapscott (1947-) Canadian business executive, author and consultant.

Social media is obviously here to stay. And when we look at a website it is usually through a link found through an internet search, or sent as a recommendation from a colleague, or by clicking through the links offered on an interesting post on one of our favourite apps. So all organisations should think carefully – if they haven't already done so – about their policies for dealing with the various technologies.

Without doubt, social media posts can also make or break the reputations of people, and even of organisations, very rapidly…

> *I'm still getting my head around social media and the continual changes. Things can go viral very quickly, especially in combination, e.g. radio with social media. You've got to have a strong strategic communications plan, that articulates where social media fits in and continually monitors activities.*

> *The traditional media cycle used to have time limits; social and online media publishing is 24 hours a day. The 'always on' nature of this platform needs to be front of mind; reputational risk can't be left for the weekend or a week while someone is on leave.*

So this means of communication must be watched carefully not only by prime users, both at 'the top' and those on the front line, but also by those involved in people management. In any event, all media (traditional or social) needs to be managed, and all organisations should regularly reflect on their policies and processes for dealing with these technologies.

The user profile of each channel really changes the way you communicate effectively, and indeed how you best engage people with your organisation and its brand. To this end, it is important to allow staff to experiment, to express personality and be 'real' in order to achieve the best engagement. It is also necessary to have enough of a social media style guide and strategy to ensure their actions are well-directed. Given the quick pace of change, mistakes will happen, but these can usually be minimised, and reduce risk with good management practices including careful oversight and systems. Noting that…

> *It can be a performance. And just as it is a different performance in talking to your peers versus lecturing in the classroom versus giving a public lecture versus appearing on radio, or TV, you have to curate it. And recognise that other people are performing too.*

The potentially positive impact of social media is really important as is keeping under review who is managing your brand and how are you are safeguarding it while maximising both the PR and other potential benefits....

> *I have a (surprising) number of followers on Twitter and use it, for example, to advertise for staff I might be looking for; or to amplify others' work; or to rebroadcast interesting stuff I've learned; or to seek help or connections. It can really be very useful.*

And while the platforms and user profiles for each social 'channel' continually change and evolve quickly, the two-way conversation also allows almost anyone and everyone to 'publish'. It also can create groups of likeminded people, and the only way to keep in touch with what your organisation cares about, or has to say, is to play in the same arena. Remembering that social media 'influencers' aren't necessarily experts, or qualified, or bound by a professional code – rather they are, more often than not, the most popular voices.

It would also be wise to develop your own strategies for dealing with unpleasantness that will arise as your own profile expands. For example ...

> *I use the Good, the Bad and the Ugly to triage where I spend my time on social media. Obviously 'the good' are where our views align well: positive network building. 'The bad' I believe are often well intentioned but ill-informed, and can usually be persuaded with solid arguments: worth investing time in. 'The ugly' (happily, generally in the minority) can be malicious and nasty and you will never win them over, so I don't waste my time trying.*

Avoidance can also be a viable approach ...

I don't tweet. I send carefully constructed emails. And I listen a lot (more!). Plus my regular videos seem to go down well: people need to see their boss.

What is important is to accept that social media cannot just be left to look after themselves. What is critical is that …

As a leader you need to cautiously interact with social media to promote and protect your organisation.

Duly recognising that …

Social networking provides a great opportunity to knowledge-share, without hierarchy or barriers, bearing in mind that professionalism is needed, as in all forms of communication.

Dealing with traditional media… We all know that the media are everywhere and that they operate with varying degrees of intrusiveness. All leaders need a well-thought-through policy for dealing with media approaches. As a general rule, when a journalist rings up, take the call – or at the very least, in order to get your head around the issues, respond with a "Give me ten minutes and I'll get back to you." And, again – make sure that you do. Within eight minutes would be better.

Journalists are sometimes inherently lazy, or very busy and time-strapped. Feed them regularly and proactively.

The media like to publish everything that is negative; but when you have something positive to tell often they're not interested.

The popular conception of academic institutions as havens of vicious conflicts is not in tune with what I experienced as a Vice-Chancellor. Of course there were conflicts… but they were never as deep and as difficult as the media tried to make them.

An enlightening observation from one journalist was "Thank you very much for talking to me; it was very helpful. If you hadn't spoken to me, I'd have probably just made up a response."

We once made the mistake of getting into an extremely confrontational relationship with a particular journalist. So much so that we eventually declined any contact, being advised "Don't give him any oxygen." This proved, in hindsight, to have been a serious error. He got his (well-polluted) 'oxygen' elsewhere. And we suffered from the 'power of the pen'.

Excellent training courses focused on dealing with the media are now available. These are usually one-on-one for senior leaders. It is a brave leader who believes that he or she has no need for advice and guidance in this area.

Media training is fundamentally important.

The Annual Report... This is a necessary evil for which the cost-benefit ratio is probably very unfavourable. Minute attention to detail is usually required – so make sure someone on your team with the necessary obsessive instincts is in charge. But top leadership time allocated to the two- to three-page overview is without doubt a good investment. This can also be a useful, and motivational, information 'circular' for the rest of your organisation and for key stakeholders, including alumni.

Take care to get the 'look and feel' right. And make copies available to everyone – it is surprising just how many people (from the 'top' to the 'bottom') like to take a copy home to show off to the family and friends – "This is where I work, and this is what we do. Pretty cool, eh?"

Death by PowerPoint?...

Power corrupts. PowerPoint corrupts absolutely.

PowerPoint is not quite as intrusive as email and obviously has widespread and useful application. But it can take on a life of its own and, in the process, create a serious dependency. In that context it is instructive to look at the spoof PowerPoint version of the Gettysburg Address (http://norvig.com/Gettysburg) – something of a cold shower for those over enthused with this form of 'communication'.

And, interestingly, Apple founder and CEO Steve Jobs evidently banned it from being used in any meeting he attended, famously saying that "People who know what they're talking about don't need PowerPoint".

For a medium that has such a dominant influence on credibility and reputation it's astounding how frequently PowerPoint presentations are undertaken so poorly.

A rhetorical question: over the past twelve months what percentage of the talks you have been to were (still) such that: (a) the technology failed (at some point); and/or (b) the slides were illegible for any normal-eyed person more than halfway back; and/or (c) if they could be read, they mostly couldn't be understood; and/or (d) the spoken and visual words bore little relationship to each other; and/or (e) the slide text was read, verbatim and boringly ("so you think I can't read?"); and/or (f) the talk was going on too long and some interesting-looking slides were jettisoned apparently at random, perhaps because of a lack of time?

The worst aspect of PowerPoint is the boring thing – but they do at least turn off the lights so you can go to sleep!

At the serious risk of our being over-prescriptive, the '6P' Rule may be helpful here: 'Planning and Preparation Prevent Pitifully Poor Performance'. This might include the potential for dry-run and feedback sessions with your harshest and most trustworthy critics.

At the end of the day – *the* leadership imperative... So, highlighting the importance of the topic of this whole section:

You have to have the ability to communicate effectively. The skill can be tuned (for improvement) but if you don't have it, things get very difficult.

Communication 'cubed' is a leadership imperative – communication, communication, communication.

10. Giving CREDIT

"I can live for a month on a good compliment." Mark Twain (1835-1910) US writer and humourist.

Our colleagues – up, down and sideways – need to be recognised and celebrated when they've done something good, or done something well. And your job, as a leader, is to do the recognising and the celebrating, in the right context and in the right way.

In terms of bringing out the best in your people, recognising contributions and giving praise and credit where it is due is one of the most powerful – and most regularly underused – of motivators. However, this must be done carefully, and well, since it can be a possible source of resentment if it is done badly, or not at all.

You need to be able to tell people honestly where they've done well. And don't give false praise. People recognise a 'snow job' in a microsecond.

Make sure your 'praising' or 'special thank you' letters don't sound like variations on a form letter with a few words made specific to the recipient. Your cats pick this kind of thing up very quickly, and their opinion of you will drop as a result. Don't wait too long to give praise. Don't think "I'll tell her later" or "I'll chat to him when the project's over". Deferred praise doesn't cut it like instant recognition does – and you might even forget. If someone does a good job, tell them now.

Awards and recognition can also be important drivers of change, and reinforce the behaviour you're seeking, for example in nurturing cross-boundary interaction or better teamwork, as well as just individual achievement.

But there is an important paradox here. Former US President Harry Truman once famously – and accurately – remarked "It is amazing what you can accomplish if you do not care who gets the credit."

However, this is a paradox because it might lead to the conclusion that assigning credit 'ownership' is unimportant. Thus, while President Truman may well have been addressing the negative consequences of jostling for credit, it is, of course, through allocated (and peer-recognised) credit that we can motivate and encourage people, secure funding, get promoted, enhance peer credibility, etc., etc. – especially in the competitive worlds of academia and research. To us, however, the important issues are the giving of credit, and ensuring that credit is not wrongly attributed. Taking the credit is not the prerogative of the leader.

> "No man will make a great leader who wants to do it all himself or get all the credit for doing it." Andrew Carnegie (1835-1919) US industrialist and philanthropist.

By the way, if you think you'll get much thanks or praise for what you have done, forget it. Most cats don't work that way. The Chinese maxim around leadership applies: "When the job gets done, the people say 'We did it ourselves'."

When someone passes off your ideas as theirs, don't worry – you've won.

The personal touch… Somehow, in the hurly-burly busy-ness of our daily lives, we often forget to acknowledge and celebrate the very many special things that happen all around us – at home, at work or in the supermarket. But when we get it right it can have tremendous impact:

More than twenty years back I can still remember my boss at the time saying "I just can't tell you how proud I am of you". A simple bit of praise, delivered with real sincerity – and showing a deep belief in me, taking me to a new level of confidence in what I could achieve – has lasted me half a working lifetime!

…the personal handwritten note, or email, can mean a lot…

Joe was a great scientist. World class, in fact. And a loyal supporter through some tough changes. Long in the tooth but short on appropriate airs and graces. And a talented enthusiast – as his wife used to say: "an adolescent trapped in an old man's body". One day I popped by his office for a chat. No pre-arrangement. To my considerable surprise, centrepiece of his pinboard was a note I had dropped him six months previously. It went along the lines of "Great job, Joe. We're proud of you. Keep up the fantastic work."

What sometimes may seem not very important to you can very often have much greater significance to those on the receiving end.

Public recognition... In the 'cats' environment, never underestimate the power of an award to show appreciation and to motivate. From 'Best Paper at the Conference' to honorary doctorates to Nobel prizes...

When it comes to recognition and awards, it's also good to make them visible, and make a fuss. And generally it's more about emotion, not about money. Acknowledgement by peers is a big deal.

Public recognition and praise for the contribution played by many people in achieving beneficial outcomes for the institution... brings out the very best in people.

But a word of caution – if it is going to be quite a long list you're acknowledging, make really sure – by double checking – that you don't miss any key contributors from that list. Elementary, you may think, but when this happens it is probably worse than giving no recognition at all.

In a group email, celebrating achievement, it is usually a mistake to single out just two or three individuals. The other forty-seven say to themselves "What about me? I work hard too!" The individual note works wonders.

Formal acknowledgement and attribution... If in doubt, err on the side of generosity when acknowledging the contributions of others in published material. There's no downside. Everyone knows who the key contributors are.

In a 'cats' environment there are not many areas where you – as a leader – need to be neurotic, and go obsessively into the detail, but acknowledging others' contributions is one, especially where text is used verbatim. Plagiarism – even a whiff of it – is a seriously dirty word, and very career-limiting. When it comes to publications, for instance, omitting a key contributor's name, whether intentionally or merely in error, generally has long-term negative consequences. So be warned.

Finally, rigorous use of alphabetical order in author attribution can confuse things – so talk it through to ensure accuracy and authenticity – and the maintenance of ongoing good relationships.

Claiming (all the) credit, and worse... There is a final point here.

Selfishness in not sharing credit can bring out the worst in people.

Further, claiming credit where it is *not* due is the leader's credibility kiss-of-death:

Thirty years' back our department head sought to muscle his name in on our work (unsuccessfully I might add, but not without some heated – and at that stage potentially career-limiting – exchanges). Even after his funeral it was a historical act of inappropriateness that still sprung to mind when his name came up. And worse – I nearly slipped into the temptation myself decades later, sheepishly apologising in horror when I realised what I was doing.

MANAGING THE PEOPLE – In Conclusion

All business is people business.

In a 'cats' environment you need to be collegiate, not commanding. And in truth the ONLY long-term, sustainable advantage for you and your organisation lies with your talented people. Handle with thought and care – and as a priority. Pursue excellence where enthusiasm and judgement also exist –

all three hand-in-hand. Interrogate track record unashamedly. Note that difficult people abound; perversely they are often the creative life blood of your operation.

More than eighty per cent of your success will depend on your ability to pick people. Getting others, whom you trust, to offer differing perspectives is usually valuable. And continue to look carefully at those who are already with you. 'New brooms' can take a lot of your time, and are not always successful.

Provide the shoulders for others to climb on – developing your star talent is too frequently neglected. You will also need to put in hard work to build your team – 'Together Everyone Achieves More'.

Be clear about performance expectations and work to improve your skills in giving feedback. But when a situation is problematic, trust your gut feelings (and experience) and don't waste too much time. More dangerously, don't duck the issue and hope the problem will go away. Help people who need to be moved on to do so, with compassion.

As a 'conductor', your leadership baton is communication excellence. All too often, communication is badly done – the root of many (probably most?) day-to-day problems in organisations. Make sure that you and your 'troops' speak the same language – remember that it is up to you to speak theirs, not vice versa. The wording you choose to use, verbally or in writing, is critical and will be closely scrutinised. Communication is especially important in an environment of change and with the explosion of social media – the reason why we choose to use 'communication cubed'. You can never do enough.

Lastly – and certainly not least – harness the much neglected motivational power of saying 'thank you' and/or 'well done', timeously and generously. A sincere, personal touch in celebration or praise giving – whether through the informal hand-written note or phone call, or appropriate 'hoopla' of well-deserved awards – is often remembered long after its origins are forgotten.

All business is people business.

D: LEADING STRATEGICALLY

Much is talked about 'strategy'. Voluminous tomes abound. The same is true of 'change'.

So, last, but very much not least, in this small 'guidebook' we have sought to address the essence – and interrelationships – of strategy and change, and the ways in which we see them as applicable to the 'business' of herding cats.

We address the need to have goals which are both stretching and inspiring – yet ultimately achievable. And making the tough choices, and focusing effort predominantly on these goals. In a nutshell, strategic planning features. As does the priority for straightforward – and repetitive – communication.

Effecting change is what good leaders do, indeed what they mostly do. Succeeding in the complex, conservative, often Machiavellian world of academia and research is hard and fraught with sophisticated opposition and risk – both personal and institutional.

We provide you with some pointers that we have found useful.

11. Strategy is about CHOICE

"The leader's role is to describe reality, and give hope."
Napoleon Bonaparte (1769-1821)

In other words…

You need to tell a realistic story about where we are, and an optimistic story of where we're headed.

Remembering…

Strategy is never meaningful unless it results in a reallocation of resources.

Focus, focus, focus… Most importantly, of the plethora of possibilities and options that will commonly open up for you, a 'focus on the few' is essential.

"It is our choices, Harry, that show who we truly are, far more than our abilities." Albus Dumbledore, Headmaster, Hogwarts School of Witchcraft in J.K. Rowling's *Harry Potter and the Chamber of Secrets* (1998).

Reflecting on what got him involved with – and, more importantly, excited by – the possibility of a career in science, Dr Ramesh Mashelkar tells another – wonderful – story. As a small boy, he was fortunate in having a teacher who was passionate about science. One day, this man took the junior physics class out into the hot Indian sun to talk about optics, measuring the focal length of lenses – you may remember the exercise: varying the distance between the lens and a piece of paper, concentrating the sun's rays to a spot. As the paper blackened and smoke formed, and with the first lick of a flame, Ramesh's teacher turned to him, looked into his eyes – looked into his soul as Ramesh describes it – and said: "See, Ramesh, look what happens when you focus your energy – you can set the world on fire. Indeed, you can set the world on fire."

Strategy is about choice. It's saying we're going to focus on these things, and not on those. This is where we are going to put our effort.

Rolling back from the future… Canada's Wayne Gretzky was, by all accounts, the greatest ever ice hockey player. In a tough, bruising, competitive sport he also earned the trophy, five times, for being 'the most gentlemanly player'. He has been cited as among the top ten greatest athletes of the twentieth century. Carrying his fans' mantle of 'The Great One' with tact and humility, he was once asked, "Why are you so good?" His reply (bear in mind that ice hockey is played with a thing called a puck) was along the lines of: "I guess that in hockey, as in life, I've always tried to focus on where the puck's gonna be, not where it is now." And that's where he skated, with great effect.

This provides in a few words the essence of good strategy – rolling backwards from the future, not extrapolating forwards from the present.

Big goals…

It's vital to be able to describe and sell the future in an inspirational way.

Creating a strategic vision requires thinking on a different scale from the day-to-day requirements of leading and managing. Your strategy must not be just a variation on the status quo. It should seek to take the organisation to a different, higher, level of performance, and stature. It should seek to galvanise and inspire:

In the research business you need to make sure you give your direct reports, or team, a really major challenge.

It's so easy to get lost in the small things. But so important – and hard – to make the big bets.

Five hundred or more years ago Michelangelo said, "The greater danger for most of us lies not in setting our aim too high and falling short, but in setting our aim too low, and achieving our mark." In the same vein, author Jim Collins in his book *Built to*

Last talks about the importance of 'BHAGs.' (verbalised as 'bee-hags') – Big Hairy Audacious Goals. Even Sir Francis Drake, the 16th-century explorer, had a relevant prayer: "Disturb us, Lord … when our dreams have come true because we have dreamed too little…"

> *We had a big game plan – to raise our ambitions, and explore uncharted territories.*

> *Trusting in our big ideas is a priority for us, and people know it.*

> *If I could go back twenty years I'd be even more ambitious.*

> *When it comes to talented people, the good news is that we're in Silicon Valley. But it's only good news if you're working on something big and important – otherwise the most talented people won't work with you; they'll go elsewhere.*

A small cautionary note, however, since there should be limits to 'bigness'. Intelligent people will recognise it immediately if your goal is completely unachievable in the time scales you set. Thereafter, you are into 'mission impossible' territory:

> *Leadership in R&D is all about credibility. You can set any stretch target and have some ideas on how to meet it, but if you set it out too far the credibility with the team is essentially zero. Equally, if you set a target which is only a marginal improvement on where you are, the inspiration to move and do things differently is again zero. It's like the old rubber band analogy: you stretch it too tight and credibility is broken; you have it too slack and there's no drive for change.*

Planning strategically… Once it has been decided that a new strategy is needed, the evolution of that strategy requires unwavering commitment. It cannot be done effectively when just squashed into the spaces of the day job. While it is unrealistic to expect the leader to drop everything to concentrate solely on strategy, he or she needs someone at their elbow who is unswervingly devoted to working with them to keep the process of strategy formulation in the forefront of activity.

So the strategic planning process itself necessarily has a beginning, a middle and an end, all of which have differing requirements.

In the academic world strategy is about differentiation. Your senior colleagues want to know what your institution can do that others can't. So you have to define that.

The start of the planning process requires a careful appraisal of the current position. Before you can decide where to go, it is necessary to know where you are. This requires definition of the so-called 'current realities':

Change starts with a frank and transparent assessment of where we are, warts and all.

However, the development of a strategy also needs to be preceded by the determination, or re-examination, of your mission and vision statements. These provide the contexts in which strategy can evolve and a strategic plan be formulated for achieving the goals that are identified, and sought. Furthermore, there should be an analysis of the broader landscape in which your strategic action is to be pursued.

Describing your current environment – technical and business – is the first priority in strategic planning. And people make assumptions, which you need to examine closely. This should be a fact-based procedure.

This part of the process will need to be followed by the planning exercise itself, which usually requires bringing together groups of staff with different responsibilities and from different levels within your organisation. The overall process is generally a formidable one, so it will usually be best – at a comparatively early stage – to seek to narrow the range of alternatives quite significantly. Decisions are usually not irreversible, and alternatives that were initially discarded can almost always be revived at a later stage. In all cases, however, there will be a need to achieve a good balance between 'top down' planning, usually led strongly by the more senior officers, and 'bottom up' planning, which allows the general cohort of staff, on whom the success of implementation will be strongly dependent, to make meaningful inputs and to feel ownership.

The skills and insights of those at the frontline are extremely valuable – and regularly and systematically disregarded by the policy makers at the top.

Stanford Professor of Management, Robert Burgelman, talks about the importance of tapping into the 'wisdom of the anthill'. In this vein, some while back, one of us was working in an environment of intense change. The organisation was getting some good help with strategy from external consultants. Six weeks into the project someone asked: "I wonder what the people think?" Lots of well-organised, energised, time-bound task groups later, we found there was essentially a one-to-one correspondence with what the consultants had come up with. (They were, after all, listening hard and consolidating.) A lesson not to be forgotten.

Proclaiming messages from the top – without getting organisation ownership of decisions taken – will lead to scepticism.

After these deliberations, the plan needs to be wrapped up in a suitable package and then communicated widely and effectively – and repeatedly:

In terms of vision and strategic development… you can never tell the story enough times, either within the institution or externally.

Here, we believe it's worth reiterating a quote we used earlier:

You must, repeat must, keep your strategic messages very clear, and few in number; very straightforward, easily understood and digestible. Use simple terms, easy to remember and to understand, and to pass on. And then repeat, repeat, repeat – be boring!

For the desk of the 'One Minute Vice-Chancellor'... A quick summary around planning strategically:

Step 1: Make a realistic – and as far as possible quantitative – assessment of your current broad environment (institution, system, country, world), and envisaged (e.g. ten-year) shifts. SWOT (Strengths/Weaknesses/Opportunities/Threats) and PEST (Political/Economic/Social/Technological) analyses can help.

Step 2: Strategic intent – where do you want to be? (Recognising, as previously mentioned, that good strategy is not rolling forward from the present, but rolling back from the future.)

Step 3: How do you get from A to B? (Choices, and prioritisation). Articulate the set of tasks and tactics, and follow through. And then, in parallel:

Step 4: Communicate, communicate, communicate – simply, and repetitively.

> *Over thirty years of practising it, I've learned three things about strategy. One: 'less is more' – drop things, and prioritise. Two: 'stay the course' – change is hard and takes time. Three: 'simplify'– plain English, repetitively, and simple models.*

> *Since taking over two years back I only talk about three things: delivering good outcomes, trusting our big ideas, and the importance of first-class talent.*

Inside help... Many universities have Business Schools in which there are first-rate staff capable of offering sound advice but they are not always recognised as the asset they can be.

> *In terms of getting good advice, I am often surprised – in the context of 'the prophet not being welcome in his own country' – that many university leaders seem sceptical about valuing, and using, the talent and experience that resides in their excellent Business Schools.*

We feel that this can be an unfortunate oversight.

Outside help, and the external perspective... There are very mixed views about the extent to which 'outside' help and advice should be a part of enabling the strategic planning process.

In the first instance, the external perspective – for example what top peers/'competitors' are doing – can provide useful insights; 'keeping up with (or ahead of?) the Joneses' can prove helpful both in getting nay-sayers on board, and in strengthening the resolve of your supporters – and providing them with some ammunition:

> *Getting some top academics from around the world to spend time with us, helping us identify weaknesses and problem areas, was really valuable. These messages were reinforced when, not inexpensively, we took the whole leadership team 'on tour', exposing them, in a concentrated fashion, to what top institutions were doing. The lights came on, and stayed on.*

When it comes to employing the official consultancy professionals, in the world of academia and research, consultants are often treated with a mixture of scepticism and suspicion:

> *Forget the old 'borrowing your watch to tell you the time' adage. These guys came in, started a fire and then got paid for putting it out!*

> *When I think about the use of consultants, I am reminded that I often found the people in our culture don't value it if someone else tells them – they should discover it themselves.*

But there is a counter view...

> *I found the use of consultants valuable in giving messages that I knew in my bones were the right ones, but needed the 'prophet from without' to articulate them.*

> *The Board were much more on side with the proposed changes with the big name consultants' thick report and PowerPoint presentations behind them.*

And further: the fresh eye from the outsider can often help you distinguish 'the wood' from 'the trees' – those 'big picture' things that get missed in the day-to-day of working life. Similarly:

> After working with the consultants, we realised we were probably moving into 'boiled frog' country: you know the old story – the frog in water that warms up gradually never jumps out, and dies. The frog who jumps into hot water, jumps out. They helped us see where the water was getting really hot.

Thus, correctly managed – repeat, correctly managed – our view is that the external perspective can add a lot of value. This can be leveraged if and when you have your own 'A-team' working closely with the external players – with a designated responsibility to oversee the implementation after the consulting assignment has formally concluded. Taking real ownership is very important in ensuring that the insights you might get from external help in crafting good strategy get properly calibrated and embedded in your organisation...

> *I see elegant strategies – developed, for example, by the very bright people the consultants brought in – falter when it comes to getting them applied in practice. The brilliant analysts who crunch the data and imagine new futures have rarely, if ever, persuaded a union official to accept substantial changes in job descriptions or job losses. They have never had to deal with the arrogance of some senior academics who always know best, or the scarred bureaucrats whose occasional experiences of moving beyond the comfort of prescribed rules and procedures have left them battered and bruised.*

In our sort of environment, where there are usually severe budgetary constraints, there are sometimes problems with employing the 'heavyweights', not least because of the expense involved. It is great to chat with the senior partner(s) doing the pitch but (sometimes) disappointing when it is the two-year-in juniors, working hundred-hour weeks, who end up doing the job. The smaller, more specialised, and usually less expensive, 'boutique' providers often have a creativity of their own and an ability to be objective. Here, what you see is very much what you get.

Managing risk… While strategy is about aspiration and intent, there is, of course, a place for formally identifying – and examining – the major risks your institution might face. That is just good leadership practice. But nowadays it seems that a whole industry has arisen around risk assessment, key threats, and the like. It has led, sadly and far too often, to a tendency for 'box ticking'. Thus:

> *You can spend an awful lot of time imagining – and documenting – the worst that can happen. It's bananas! Very often you just have to manage the things that arise, as best you can.*

> *Most of the nuts and bolts stuff around risk we did (just) for the benefit of the Risk Committee.*

> *You need to apply healthy common sense. And not slavishly obey the professional advice you get given. And understand, for example, especially with your lawyers and contract people, where they are coming from, which is often a position of total risk aversion.*

> *Every leadership job will have crises. And typically not the crises that you can anticipate. They just fall out of the sky.*

But be forewarned and forearmed: some thoughtful reflection around the risks you might encounter on your strategic journey can be a positive aid to your strategic planning. As a Sony executive once recounted to us, far from arrogantly, "The future will never surprise us – we've already been there."

> *One can be too dismissive of risk management. It can of course be (and often is) a box-ticking exercise. But it should not be. At its best it can be a very positively structured way of understanding the strengths and weaknesses of strategy.*

Needless to say, your biggest risks are likely to be people-related.

Either losing talent key to your progress and success, or poor decisions or behaviours that can adversely affect your institution's reputation and your own legacy. Or, as previously mentioned, putting too many of your 'eggs' (strategic initiatives) in a single basket. Vigilance is therefore critical, especially where there are deep-seated cultural issues at play.

When you identify a potentially damaging risk, it's really important to move on it fast; talk about it openly and transparently with close colleagues, including communicating 'up the chain'. Sitting on your hands and hoping it will go away – perhaps because it can be tough to manage undesirable behaviours – is rarely a good option.

On leading, and managing, in a crisis…

Managing in a crisis? What's new? When have we not been managing in some crisis or other?

So said a senior university executive we spoke to on this topic. Maybe this attitude is not too common, but common enough, we are sure, to raise a smile with many of our readers!

Crises can come suddenly, or creep up on you over time (because they're not recognised early enough, or ignored and not dealt with). They can be short- or long-lived. And 'big' – potentially affecting the whole of the organisation, and beyond – or modest in scale, and more manageable.

But the leader carries the proverbial can. Action – strategically, and operationally – is essential.

How did I manage and lead in the crisis, and what did I learn? A crisis brings out the best – and the worst – in people. Beware the panic merchants. So… 1. I took it seriously and dealt with it as soon as possible. 2. I put the best person I could find in charge. And took her off-line (and back filled). 3. I enhanced communication. She and her team met daily, first thing, and I was available to her 24/7. And I listened carefully (not normally my strong suit!). And I didn't tweet but sent regular emails, and did weekly videos, both uploaded straight to our website. It went well.

Let us say it again, you have got to stay closely in touch, at *both* strategic and operational levels…

In a crisis, the advice "don't sweat the small stuff" is bad advice. Suggesting that senior leaders should 'look after strategy' and others, 'lower down', should look after the 'management', can result in bad mistakes. The devil really is in the detail. And keep asking questions.

As we have described elsewhere, clarity of roles and responsibilities is critical…

In a crisis I believe in collaborative leadership but this doesn't mean that everyone is equally responsible, and accountable. You must always clarify, and document, exactly who is on the line for what component of your implementation actions. And follow up.

Because failing to do so can lead to real problems…

Observing the way that the crisis was managed presented the worst example of mismanagement that I've seen… half a dozen good, willing people with overlapping responsibilities. Progress was a mess.

Major crises can also really test your communication and people skills…

Stay composed, and speak with as much candour as you can: what I know, what I don't know, and what I am committed to doing.

As a leader you need to be careful, as you probably know more about what's going on, and have perhaps become inured to the shock. But your staff might feel destabilised and frightened by all the ambiguity. You need to try and help people find a safe harbour.

Now as we have said before, the leadership job – especially in a crisis situation – can be lonely, and really tough on you personally.

My job is to try to absorb uncertainty and stop my people from feeling scared. But in so doing you need to engage in more self-care. You're probably the custodian of the most knowledge and are trying to protect your people. Carrying their anxieties can be exhausting.

When things evolve in a way which isn't what you expected or anticipated, and new information comes to light, and different decisions are required, you need to be honest in apologising, with candour and courage. Part company with your ego and embarrassment!

But there can also be real upsides...

A crisis can be a gift for a leader. It dissolves away any lack of clarity around priorities. But it still needs courage to push what's really needed.

A crisis can facilitate agility, and your ability to take bold, decisive action. It can give you a real opportunity to push through some out-of-the-box ideas.

And we have all observed how a major, nations-wide health crisis can unleash, and indeed has unleashed, unprecedented collaboration and information sharing – with corresponding vastly accelerated scientific progress – at a scale and at pace not seen before.

The need for cybersecurity is growing... Sadly, one of the increasingly prevalent risks that leaders in academic and research organisations – and indeed, most organisations – must deal with is that of cybersecurity. Many of us have heard, in this context, the view that 'there are only two types of companies: those that have been hacked; and those that have been hacked and don't (yet) know it!'

Indeed, in recent times, the escalation of working from home has necessarily increased the importance of – and complexity around – cybersecurity issues more than ever before. Such attacks can be truly significant. For example, Professor Brian Schmidt is a Nobel Laureate and Vice-Chancellor of the Australian National University which suffered a couple of major cyber attacks. Professor Schmidt admits to being less concerned about state-backed hackers than about cybercriminals, saying, "If it is a state-run actor they're kind of nice inside your domains; they don't destroy things. But if you get criminals in there, they hold you hostage and they literally can destroy the enterprise."

Fixing it is no easy (or cheap) task, but can produce positive improvements; as he adds: "Having dealt with the first attacks, thereafter by building up our capability (and appointing top notch cybersecurity professionals), we were suddenly able to detect things that, quite frankly, we had never been able to detect in the past."

Communication is (again) key, as researchers may push back on necessary controls that are implemented, complaining – if they are not well informed – that this limits their ability to use software they need, or carry out experiments they want to run.

And, again, forewarned is forearmed…

> Problems can come post crisis, or with 'prolonged crisis' which can merge into a form of perceived dictatorship. New-found leadership freedoms introduced in crisis are not always willingly given up and, correspondingly, in prolonged crisis, stress levels rise: depression/anxiety are infectious in groups, and future angst becomes inhibitory to current work.

Above all, in managing the potential risks inherent in any crisis situation, it's important to remember that…

> In a crisis, evaluation shouldn't happen at the end. It needs to be a very regular exercise. Learning by doing and then actioning that learning, in real time, is so critical.

12. Leading and managing CHANGE

"Even if you are on the right track, you will get run over if you just sit there." Will Rogers (1879-1935) American film actor.

Whether it's based on strategic thinking or simply arises as a result of external circumstance, change is ever present and inevitable in both the academic and the research domains.

Change must be led and must be managed.

Leadership implies change. Good leaders take what is not working, or not working well, and change it so that it works better.

Powerful speeches and fine rhetoric don't (often) change culture – you need structure and process to deliver culture change, and embed it.

Robust thought and dialogue – the bread and butter of academia – is often a major prerequisite for important change in our world. But just try to get the average academic to even shift offices.

Change is great so long as someone else is changing.

As a senior colleague painfully summarised, "The university is a strange beast – organic and chaotic – and bringing about change can be a tricky exercise. The ability to ignore and push back is immense".

And change is hard…

The analysis and high-level decisions behind strategy never fully account for the blood, sweat and toil in getting change implemented and getting people to do things differently.

Even the best leaders have often been away from the coalface so long that they forget the realities of getting apprehensive and insecure people, tired and frightened of change, and deeply sceptical of the motivations (and competence) of senior management, to do things they're not used to. It is messy and difficult and often only partially successful. But it is leadership in action.

Resistance... In any change initiative, one of the most difficult tasks is getting 'buy in', and trying to promulgate a sense of ownership:

After a thirty-year career in the organisation, one of the most senior bureaucrats – at his farewell dinner – bemoaned how hard it was to embed new ways of doing things. "The people are like seaweed," he reflected, "just keep your head down, they say, and it will all wash over you, as will the next wave."

In an early meeting with some of my most distinguished and long-serving 'cats' the essence was: "Well, you seem like a pretty good guy, you may even be better than your predecessors, but in due course you will leave and we will still be here." The feeling expressed was that new management is a temporary disturbance to the smooth running of the organisation.

Universities and the like are incredibly resistant to change. Far more so than in business or government. I believe that it is because of the focus on individual excellence – they're independent beings, and there's little collaboration, and people generally don't feel part of an 'organisation'. So you have to start early in people's careers, supporting and rewarding and promoting collaborative behaviour and team playing, building a sense of pride in the organisation as a whole. And we need to train the next generation differently, to go out there and be reformers.

Niccolò Machiavelli was a great herder of cats. His comments are as relevant today as they were in 1532:

"It ought to be remembered that there is nothing more difficult to take in hand, more perilous to conduct, or more uncertain in its success, than to take the lead in the introduction of a new order of things. Because the innovator has for enemies all those who have done well under the old conditions, and lukewarm defenders in those who may do well under the new…"

And be warned: those enemies of change can get very energised, and well organised…

Whenever something happens, or is planned, or is only just being seriously talked about, the 'old boys' network' gets unleashed and I'll get thirty letters from around the world saying what a bad idea it is and how life as we know it will surely come to an end if it happens.

Listen carefully… The reasons for change may be self-evident to you as the leader, but this clarity, more often than not, does not penetrate far down into your organisation. Thus, before change is initiated, a period of careful and sensitive listening should be the rule not the exception:

I first ask "What do we want to change, and why?" Then I urge a new leader to consult, consult, consult; listen and learn before acting on the change you want to enact.

In the first three months of a new job you mostly need to be listening, across all levels in your organisation. You need to make sure you're familiar with your environment before embarking on change.

Consultation is the basis for all good decisions and, therefore, open your door to all the stakeholders in these decisions.

I took on a top job on 1 March. On 2 March I contacted the senior 250 people across the organisation with four questions. 1. What are the three most important things we should be doing? 2. What are our most important challenges and opportunities? 3. How can we strengthen our linkages across the organisation? 4. How do we retain, develop and recruit the best talent? I later opened this up to all staff, and we got some great feedback and ideas.

Think carefully… Change consumes a lot of energy. As the old marriage service used to remind us, it is not to be taken on "unadvisedly, lightly, or wantonly". It is, therefore, important to identify – and separate out – those parts that aren't broken and don't need radically changing from those that are, and do. As Lucius Cary, Lord Falkland, said in 1641 (it's often erroneously attributed to John F. Kennedy): "When it is not necessary to change, it is necessary not to change."

For the things that aren't broken, but can still be improved, you don't need to turn the whole organisation on its head.

Next time around I definitely wouldn't embark on changing so many things at the same time. I'd plan better and take more consideration of individuals' capacity to absorb and cope.

We need to be aware that change is really threatening for many people. So you need to address the 'soft' issues of feelings and anxiety as much as the 'hard' issues of resources and the implementation timetable.

Beware the 'big bang'… Although it can be tempting, and sometimes advantageous, to bring about change as quickly as possible – and all at once, to 'get it over with' – this can have unintended, negative consequences. Erring on the side of caution can have beneficial effects, both in embedding the changes and in making them more palatable to those affected.

Evidently seafaring explorers of old, before setting out on a voyage into the unknown (not a bad metaphor for some change programmes!) would first 'port-hop' along familiar coastlines to test out their ship, their tools and their team:

Piloting was very important. We took the feedback, refined the approach and then rolled the changes out through the organisation.

"Before anything else, preparation is the key to success."
Alexander Graham Bell (1847-1922)

On the other hand, being too cautious brings with it the dangers of paralysis by analysis – 'fiddling while Rome burns', so to speak. People do need to sense the urgency. Also, perceptions that consultation is going to be 'continuous' allows well-organised rearguard actions to be set up, aimed at preserving the status quo. Therefore:

> *Once the way forward is clear, be decisive. People generally want to feel positive about their work – give them the opportunity to do so by making the tough decisions quickly.*

Here we have another paradox which requires experience and judgement if it is to be overcome effectively.

> *When I started, I was given two pieces of advice by other VCs. One group said that it was essential that that I make all the major changes in my first year, as after that nothing much would happen. Another group told me, with equal belief, that I should not rush into change and, whatever I did, not to change too much in Year 1. I made up my own mind.*

Anticipation… In some cases the change that you are seeking to bring about will also have been foreseen by (at least) the more perceptive of your colleagues, and enlisting them to facilitate the process can have advantages.

> *As Darwin said, it is not the strongest of the species that survives, nor the most intelligent; it is the one that is most adaptable to change. Going further than Darwin, I think it's fair to say that only those who can anticipate the change can lead the change.*

> "Look for intelligence and judgment and, most critically, a capacity to anticipate, to see around corners." General Colin Powell (1937-) former US Secretary of State.

Support for change… When you get seriously engaged in taking change forward it can be valuable to have a 'lead agent', someone totally and full-time engaged in leading and facilitating the change process.

That said:

> *If you appoint a radical agent for change you must also ensure that there is elbow room for them to bring the change about. Support from above is essential, and a sufficient level of support to ensure that people know it's serious.*

Equally, however, if the change agent (who may well be you) does not have real, and visible support from above, then you will largely be wasting your time. Find a new passion, or a new organisation.

Communication clarity…

> *In times of difficulty or change, a lack of frequent and straightforward communication about either the challenges facing an organisation or the roadmap for change breeds uncertainty. Uncertainty of this nature destroys focus, productivity and commitment.*

The reasons for introducing changes need to be very evident, particularly to senior leadership, but also at grassroots level. Further, you need to be crystal clear about where you're headed. The key task of leadership (along with a positive and constructive mindset) is to articulate and communicate clearly, using simple, straightforward, easy-to-remember – and few – messages.

> *Change is spelt: communicate, communicate, communicate.*

> *Get the language right. If you present in a way they don't understand, there are dangers. Especially beware 'management speak'.*

> *Once, in building the case for change, I made a blunder by quoting management guru Tom Peters' "If it ain't broke, break it" – talking about the need to 'reinvent' one's own business to stay alive in an intensely competitive, commercial environment. This went down like a lead balloon in our place.*

An important part of the message is also to build on the past, as positively as you can.

> *You need to recognise the place from whence they've come, and acknowledge what had been achieved. Just because change is now needed, doesn't mean they failed personally.*

And remember the Golden Rule:

> *He who has the gold makes the rules.*

In practice, this usually means…

> *Your most important – and perhaps your only – tool for change is creative, temporary cross-subsidy. Both adjectives are essential. This is a radically non-heroic proposition, but it works.*

> *Put out the cream, and they'll come.*

Managing – and especially managing change – is a long-haul trip. As such, in 'sticking to the game plan', managing for continuity and succession should be in the job plan for at least the 'second hundred days' of the senior change leader. Regrettably, most often it isn't.

In summary… One of the best (and simplest) articulations of effective change management we have encountered comes from Oren Harari of the Graduate School of Business in the University of San Francisco. In his book, *Leapfrogging the Competition*, he advocates '**U2D2**' guidance: ensuring that there is a clear and widespread **U**nderstanding of the need for change, and clarity about the **D**irection in which you're headed; that it always takes longer than you think, and people can get deflected or bored – therefore keep the **U**rgency button on; and a day-in, day-out **D**iscipline of ensuring well-planned execution excellence, with clear accountabilities and agreed delivery on the action steps.

LEADING STRATEGICALLY – In Conclusion

Strategy should get you from where you are now to where you want to be. Both of these positions need to be clearly articulated – your 'current reality' and your (hopefully) inspiring 'vision' of the future. Choices need to be made between the possible alternative futures; and you will have to prioritise the actions you need to take in moving you from your inherited present to your envisaged future.

Aim high, but ensure that your targets are actually achievable, and you will get (good) stretch from your people. Indeed your people, correctly engaged, can also be a great source of wisdom in contributing to defining the future that you – and, with luck, they – wish to create. Listen to them.

Nothing will happen, however, unless resources (money and time) are allocated – or reallocated – to your strategic priorities. And little will happen if you don't pay sufficient attention to ensuring clear and widespread understanding of your chosen direction, and the reasons for it – laid out in clear, concise and straightforward terms and reinforced repetitively, and over the long haul.

Key risks do need to be carefully considered, especially, and increasingly, cybersecurity risks. But too much attention (or paranoia) around 'risk' can also engender aversion and a lowering of your sights and, in turn, a loss of energy and enthusiasm. Equally, crises can spell danger, but also opportunity; proactive leadership and communication-on-steroids are essentials here.

Inevitably, your strategy will lead to change; indeed it may well be itself transformational in spirit. But change is hard work and requires careful forethought, detailed planning and – if you can – piloted implementation.

As we have said, 'communication cubed' (C3) – before, during and after – is a prerequisite for success.

POSTSCRIPT – A CLOSING THOUGHT

Finally, the essence of leading strategically and managing effectively in a 'cats' environment was aptly summarised by one of our colleagues:

I reckon there are five key dimensions to leadership in a research and development or academic environment...

1. As a research leader you must have a vision of where you want the organisation to go – because, if you don't, no one else will.

2. You articulate it, and communicate it well, to get your people excited.

3. You hire the best people you can find.

4. You create the environment where they can excel and succeed.

5. You get out of the way.

* * * *

And here are our suggestions for your corresponding **'Checklist'**:

Culture: passionate, argumentative, political, often closely tied to institutional history and flavoured with bureaucracy. Embed progress (and 'change') in history. And red-tape vigilantes can do well. If you're not comfortable leading in this type of environment, look elsewhere. It won't change in the foreseeable future.

Conflict: the 'bread and butter' of the cats community, often trivial in nature (and in perceived consequence) but potentially incendiary in emotion. Handle with care, tact and time. There are ALWAYS (at least) two sides to every story.

Collaboration: impeded by tradition, performance metrics and many common organisational systems. But it is the future, and interfaces are 'where all the exciting innovations happen'. Look for (personal) boundary-crossing opportunities and promote effective 'collabronauts'.

Charge (the taking of): mobility rules – be 'out and about'; credibility is your passport; and clear – and well-communicated – goals are your focus. Manage your time, yourself and your stakeholders, overtly. Trust your intuition, but prepare thoughtfully. Expect some failures, and take responsibility. Don't vacillate.

Composure: needed under pressure – which there will always be. Plan well, stick to your guns and obsess around effective implementation. Follow-up is essential, including around the detail.

Committees: necessarily what is needed to get quite a lot of things done, well or badly, but they are no substitute for managing through people. Ask: do you need one? Is the brief tight? Are the documents (inputs and outputs) concise? Have you got the best Chair you can find?

Cash: makes the world go around. Often your only tool for effecting change. ALWAYS never enough. Make yourself financially literate, use skilled help and seek access to some 'discretionary dollars'.

Colleagues: don't think 'subordinates'. Talent management (with strategy) should top your job list. Seek out excellence and enthusiastic spirits. Build trust (it takes TIME), quit when it is absent. Hone your juggling skills for the task/team/ individual balancing act. Delegate (at double the level you first thought of) but with crystal clear accountabilities – with follow-up. Become excellent at giving feedback and at managing performance. Beware divisions between line and support staff. All business is people business.

Communication: The cornerstone of leadership!! Poor communication is ubiquitous. And (your) actions speak louder than words. Think through your email and social media strategies (develop them if you don't already have them). Gain skills in being comfortable with the media, both social and traditional. Communicate before, communicate during, communicate after.

Credit: remember the important sentiment about 'living comfortably for a month on a good compliment'. The personal touch has real power and is often underutilised.

Choice: what 'strategy' is all about. This, not that. Rolling backwards from the future you have envisioned, not extrapolating forwards from the present you have inherited. And the need to articulate honestly. Think big, with stretch, but ultimately with achievability. It won't be a strategy unless resources shift.

Change: probably why you're doing this job – the status quo was unsatisfactory to you. Support may, especially at first, be lukewarm. Resistance will be determined, and probably well organised. Be very clear about the direction in which you're headed, and why. Communicate obsessively. Focus on the few, key 'strategic messages' – very simple, very clear and often repeated. Plan and manage tightly around execution. Act with urgency.

Once they've decided they like you, cats make good companions.

INDEX

About the Authors

Geoff Garrett...

was Queensland Chief Scientist from 2011 to 2016, having completed eight years as Chief Executive of Australia's Commonwealth Scientific and Industrial Research Organisation (CSIRO), one of the world's largest and most diverse national research organisations.

Before joining CSIRO, Geoff led South Africa's national science agency, the CSIR, as President and Chief Executive from 1995, following five years as Executive Vice President: Operations. He was named South Africa's 'Boss of the Year' in 1998, and, in that same year, 'Engineer of the Year' by the South African Society of Professional Engineers.

Educated in the United Kingdom, Geoff is a graduate of Cambridge University, where he completed a doctorate in metallurgy, and laboured hard on the cricket field under his captain, Graeme Davies. He was also a university boxing blue. He then took up a lecturing position at the University of Cape Town, and, prior to joining the CSIR, was Professor and Head of Department at the University of the Witwatersrand in Johannesburg. He held visiting positions at Brown University (RI, USA), and at Oxford and Sheffield Universities in the UK. His research interests centred around the fracture and fatigue behaviour of engineering materials.

Currently he lectures in leadership and change management

and provides coaching support in these areas to academics and to senior officers of the Australian Public Service. He is also presently Deputy Chair of the National Youth Science Forum and the Patron of the Australian Citizen Science Association.

Geoff is a Fellow of the Australian Academy of Technology and Engineering, the Royal Society of South Africa and the Australian Institute of Company Directors, and served on the Prime Minister's Science, Engineering and Innovation Council in Australia for eight years. He was also, for six years, Chairman of ANZIC, the Australia-New Zealand Consortium – comprising 20 collaborating institutions – of the major 23-country International Ocean Discovery Program, IODP. A recipient of the Centenary Medal for service to Australian society through science, Geoff was named by the Australian Financial Review as one of Australia's 2008 'True Leaders'. In June 2008 he was appointed as an Officer of the Order of Australia (AO) in the Queen's Birthday Honours list.

He is married to Janet, and they have four sons, Ben, Matt, David and Luke. His interests include fishing, tennis and table tennis, and his five (so far!) grandchildren Liam, Aran, Evie, Frankie and Reuben.

Graeme Davies...

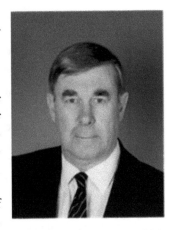

is Emeritus Vice-Chancellor of the University of London, a post he held from 2003 to 2010, following eight years as Principal of the University of Glasgow. He was Chief Executive of the Higher Education Funding Council for England from 1991 until 1995, after having been Vice-Chancellor of the University of Liverpool from 1986 to 1991. He was awarded a knighthood in the Queen's January 1996 Honours List for his services to higher education.

Sir Graeme is currently Chancellor and Chairman of the British University Vietnam in Hanoi. He is a Board Member/ Trustee of the University of Lincoln, Regent's University London, Taylor's University, Kuala Lumpur and the British Institute for Technical Education, London. He has held visiting professorships in New Zealand, Brazil, China, Argentina, South Africa, Israel and India.

Born in New Zealand, Graeme's tertiary education was with the School of Engineering of the University of Auckland, where he studied aeronautical engineering, and gained a PhD in materials science – and was a University of New Zealand football blue. A materials engineer by subsequent training and practice, he has published widely, primarily in the fields of solidification and deformation, and is the author or co-author of eight books. He was Professor of Metallurgy and Head of Department at the University of Sheffield from 1977 to 1986, having taken up that post after sixteen years in the Department of Metallurgy and Materials Science at the University of Cambridge, where he gained an MA and a ScD, and where he was also a Fellow of St Catharine's College.

Graeme is a Fellow of the Royal Academy of Engineering and a Fellow of the Royal Society of Edinburgh. He is also an Honorary Fellow of the Royal Society of New Zealand, and holds honorary degrees from thirteen universities.

He has two children, Michael and Helena, and six grandchildren. He is married to Svava Bjarnason who worked as a Principal Education Specialist in the World Bank Group. His interests include bird-watching, cricket and doing *The Times* and *The Spectator* crosswords.

About the Publisher

Triarchy Press is a small independent publisher of books that bring a wider, systemic or contextual approach to many different areas of life, including:

- Government, Education, Health and other public services
- Ecology, Sustainability and Regenerative Cultures
- Leading and Managing Organizations
- Psychotherapy and Arts and other Expressive Therapies
- The Money System
- Walking, Psychogeography and Mythogeography
- Movement and Somatics
- Innovation
- The Future and Future Studies

For books by Barry Oshry, John Seddon, Nora Bateson, Daniel Wahl, Russ Ackoff, Phil Smith, Bill Tate, Sandra Reeve, Graham Leicester, Alyson Hallett and other remarkable writers, please visit:

www.triarchypress.net

Lightning Source UK Ltd.
Milton Keynes UK
UKHW021246130521
383658UK00006B/282